The Chicken Chronicles

Also by Alice Walker

The Chicken Chronicles

Sitting With the Angels Who Have Returned
With My Memories
Glorious, Rufus, Gertrude Stein, Splendor,
Hortensia, Agnes of God, the Gladyses,
& Babe

A MEMOIR

Alice Walker

Weidenfeld & Nicolson
London

First published in Great Britain in 2011 by Weidenfeld & Nicolson
An imprint of The Orion Publishing Group Ltd
Orion House, 5 Upper Saint Martin's Lane
London WC2H 9EA

An Hachette UK Company

1 3 5 7 9 10 8 6 4 2

A CIP catalogue record for this book is
available from the British Library.

Printed in Great Britain
by CPI Mackays

The Orion Publishing Group's policy is to use papers
that are natural, renewable and recyclable products and made
from wood grown in sustainable forests. The logging and
manufacturing processes are expected to conform to the
environmental regulations of the country of origin.

www.orionbooks.co.uk

To my Mendocino familia: Laura, Efrain, Kervin, Jonathan, and Toby Balandran-Garcia; and G. Kaleo Larson, Surprise, and Miles. I am grateful for your ever-present tenderness, thoughtfulness, and love. And especially to my "girls" who, simply by being, have greatly soothed and expanded my heart.

Drink deeply. Live in serenity and joy.

Buddha

Contents

Acknowledgments

I wish to thank Marc Favreau of The New Press for wishing to publish "The Chicken Chronicles" while they were still being written on my blog, and to thank my agent Wendy Weil for asking if they could be extracted from the blog long before I had considered this.

It has been a delight working with both of you on this project, knowing that we are, however humanly fallible, seeking a more compassionate world for those who have been, especially in the last fifty years, primarily objects of ridicule and previously unimagined cruelty. We can only offer what we have, and we have this. However imperfect, may it be of use in easing a suffering—endured by other beings whose lives often sustain ours—that is so common it has become almost impossible for humans to grasp.

May our call be from this day onward, to all the creatures and beings of the planet who have no voice: I have come to you, for you, to be a witness to your life and to extend whatever understanding and happiness I can.

The Chicken Chronicles

1

PAX AMERAUCANA,
OR THE CHICKEN CHRONICLES

ONE AFTERNOON, I noticed, as if for the first time, a chicken and her brood crossing the path in front of me. She was industrious and quick, focused and determined. Her chicks were obviously well provided for and protected under her care. I was stopped in my tracks, as if I had never seen a chicken before. And in a way, I hadn't. Though I grew up in the South where we raised chickens every year, for meat and for eggs, and where, from the time I was eight or nine, my job was to chase down the Sunday dinner chicken and wring its neck. But had those chickens been like this one? Why hadn't I noticed? *Had I noticed?*

Years went by. As they do.

Once I stopped moving about quite so much my interest in chickens, and memory about that particular chicken, asserted itself. I realized I was concerned about chickens, as a Nation, and that I missed them. (Some of you will want to read no further.) I also realized I ate so many eggs, I should get to know the chickens laying them. Whenever I visited someone with chickens that they tended with respect, I felt reassured. I wanted chickens of my own.

One night at dinner with the Garcia-Balandrans, a young couple and their sons who are my neighbors, I broached the subject of my longing. The youngest boy's eyes glowed at the mention of chickens, which I thought a good sign. He is five. The older boy, nine, seemed interested as well. Their parents and I, and my partner, theorized about how to handle the logistics of raising chickens for their eggs, and of course, sharing the eggs. At first we thought we'd have a cage on wheels that we could drive back and forth from my house to theirs, letting the chickens fertilize our respective gardens on a rotational basis. We soon dropped this idea because it seemed cumbersome and messy. Plus we both have raised beds. What we decided might work would be for them to get the chickens started, when they were chicks, and then transfer them to my place when a chicken house I was dreaming of building had been completed.

This actually happened.

The boys loved the chickens and enjoyed caring for them. By midsummer when the beautiful chicken condo was ready for occupants, more chicks had been ordered to raise at their house, and their parents had bought them a dog. The day of transfer was joyful. Everyone loved the chicken house and yard, right next to my garden, so the chickens would have plenty of fresh produce, and admired the spacious interior of the chicken house, its roosts and its laying nests, which I had lovingly and with hopefulness filled with straw.

Sitting on the ground inside the chicken yard, I was astounded when a chicken strolled over and hopped up into my lap. The boys had interacted with the chickens so tenderly that they had no fear of humans. Instead this one sat very still, as I instinctively cradled it and began to coo and stroke its reddish-colored feathers. I instantly named her Gertrude, and later would call her by her full name: Gertrude Stein.

She looked nothing like Gertrude Stein, of course, but I found whenever I called her Gertrude (I soon abandoned "Gerty") the Stein naturally followed. Over the next few weeks there would be Babe, Babe II, Hortensia, Splendor, Glorious, Rufus, and Agnes of God, to name a few.

WHO KNEW WHAT WOULD HAPPEN NEXT?

WHO KNEW WHAT would happen next? Who could guess? That I would fall headlong into a mystery. That I would find myself pulled into the parallel universe that all the other animals exist in, simultaneous with us. In other words, before a couple of days had passed, watering and feeding the chickens, I had fallen in love with them. They were so undeniably gorgeous, their feathers of gold and orange and black, the designs on them. I couldn't believe I had gone years without seeing such extravagance of wearable art. And of course

I did not know who they were. I asked E.G., who calls me Mom. I call him *Hijo*. Son. *Hijo, how did you manage to find such beautiful chickens?* He shrugged: *Well, Mom, I just said five of these and six of those and three of the other guys.* And it was true, they were different. The Barred Rocks were black and white and I'd seen their kind before. There were three of them, already aggressive and jumpy; we thought they'd turn into roosters. The others though, who seemed dressed to dazzle?

I looked on the Internet (another dazzling creation: the thing most like the wonder and spontaneity of Nature, it seems to me, that humans have conjured): there are so many kinds of chickens! Who knew? Growing up, my mother had mostly ordered, from the Sears and Roebuck catalog, Rhode Island Reds.

At first, going by their feathers, I thought they might be Araucanas, a South American breed. But it turned out those chickens are rumpless. Imagine. And that the people who raise them like this because . . . without a rump it is harder for creatures, in the jungle and out, to catch them. This is too basic. Anyway, looking further, I saw the tufted ear feathers, the glowing, perfectly variegated back and tail feathers that my new chickens were sporting. They were Ameraucanas, and apparently, among other wonders, they lay blue and green eggs. Aquarians love these colors. But for eggs,

I have to say, I've always preferred brown. It's content of character though, as we know.

Years ago I had bought a tiny metal stool and for a good twenty-five years never had time to sit on it. I had painted it green, though, with a bit of hope. I found it, placed it in a corner of the chicken yard, and sat.

They were making a sound I hadn't heard since childhood, maybe infancy, and had forgotten. A kind of *queraling* (I made up this word because that's what the sound is like: part chortle, part quarrel). When I offered cracked corn they crowded round and ate it from my hands. When done, the one I would name Babe jumped into my lap, much to the interest of Gertrude Stein who considered my other knee also a lap. They liked to roost, I saw, and chose any elevation above the ground: the garbage cans in which their food is stored, the water dispenser, the roosting bars that I made from a few odd sticks. Babe settled into my arms (Gertrude S. having hopped away in search of a bug) like she'd always been there, drowsy and quiet, as if she were a cat.

Who knew?

3

FOUR BROWN EGGS!
YAAY, SPACE NUTS! *

SO I STROLLED down the hill to see the girls; as I try to do every day. It's been raining a lot, with wind, and I've spent more than a little time sleeping. Glorious. I called out to them, as I do: *Hi, Girls, it's Mommy.* They

---

* *Space Nuts.* I coined this expression—and use it a lot—to apply to the human race. Here we are hurtling through space so fast we're not even aware of it, and doing some extraordinarily unhelpful things. Fighting each other, murdering the planet, eating extremely bad food, lying about everything, and so on.

rushed to the fence, as they always do, and I counted them, as I always do; then I informed them, which they've heard before, that I was going to get a special treat for them. Today it was apples. I went over to a tree, shook it, and brought the apples back in my basket and tossed them across their straw-littered and scratched-up yard. I picked some outrageously healthy kale that seemed about to swallow its bed and tossed that in too. I then took up the rusty metal spatula that I use to scrape away poop—from food cans and water dispenser and especially from the "porches" to their nests inside—and I opened the people-sized door that leads into their dwelling. Their house smells sweet, which amazes me every time. It smells sweet, because

---

Then there are the good things: we try to stop war; we take care of Mother Earth as best we can; we pay attention to what goes into our precious, once in this lifetime, bodies. We honor Truth. *Yaay, Space Nuts!*

Or sometimes instead of *Yaay, Space Nuts!* One would say, *Aw, Space Nuts.* Or simply *Space Nuts* and the intonation of the voice would do the work. Former president Bush was a *Space Nut.* One would not say, *Yaay.* Just: *Space Nut.* Aung San Suu Kyi, the Dalai Lama, Amma, Jesus, Buddha, John Lewis, Rudolph Byrd, Beverly Guy-Sheftall and Valerie Boyd, Garrett Kaleo Larson and Che Guevara would be *Space Nuts* and we would say, *Yaay.* Etc. Etc. Maybe this expression replaces the earlier much used *My people, my people!*

of the hay that covers the washable concrete floor and fills the nests, and because of the lumber used to build everything, and because their poop is basically from fruit and vegetable matter. I treasure the poop and always praise and thank them for it. In the spring, after winter composting (maybe two winters because chicken poop is so hot) it will go on the vegetable beds. *We have a working team here*, I often tell them.

Well, yes, OK. I imagine them responding. *But what's with the tasteless worms you've got crawling out of your shoes?* It is incredible to me that they've never seen a worm, yet because my shoelaces resemble worms they will peck at them until they occasionally untie both my shoes.

So there I am with my rusty spatula, scraping their poop off their porches, and from inside their nests as well, when what do I see: four small light-brown eggs. I can't believe it. Perfectly formed, clean as a whistle. A bit of straw and a tiny wispy feather stuck to one egg, but that was it. *Yaay, Space Nuts!* I cried. They all crowded around the door as if to witness my response. *Thank you, thank you, thank you!* I said, letting a favorite feeling, astonishment, wash over me. *This is the best gift of all. You have given us these four beautiful eggs. What wonderful people you are. Chicken people*, I stressed, to discourage any thought of human arrogance. They seemed pleased.

But who was responsible? Not the Ameraucanas, because the eggs were not green or blue. Maybe the Barred Rocks, Rufus and Agnes, whom I took to be roosters? Or maybe the youngish-looking Rhode Island Reds?

But we are getting ahead of ourselves.

Back on the green stool in the corner of the chicken yard, earlier in the summer, I am noticing what chickens, with plenty of space and good food and fresh air, like to do.

4

WHAT DO CHICKENS LIKE TO DO?

THEY LIKE TO take naps! I would not have believed it if I hadn't seen it with my own eyes. Not only do they like to take naps, they like to take naps together. They especially like to take naps in the afternoon when the weather is hot. This summer there were many very hot days: 105 to 110. I've learned the trick of jumping in the pond with my clothes on and leaving them on to dry. Cheap air conditioning. Or, I will lie in a hammock in the shade with a wet towel for a sheet. Or lie in the bathtub filled with cold water, reading.

The chickens, though, burrow into the earth as far as they can, kicking aside the straw, and they will make a circle of their special friends, and they will slowly nod off. It is enchanting to watch them do this. There will be the most sumptuous quiet, as if the whole world feels drowsy. It would be difficult to imagine war and terror anywhere on Earth. It is too hot, in any case, to think of it. They also like to preen themselves; for this they will fluff out their feathers and peck around under them, shaking out loose feathers, dust, and vermin as they go.

I placed our chicken house on a slight slope, facing east so that sunlight floods the upper ventilation windows in the morning and splashes across their ascending and descending ladder and their tiny front door. A maple I planted fifteen years ago gives shade over their dining area; when it is very hot, they congregate here; filling up the roosting sticks and slipping and sliding around the slippery tops of the garbage (food storage) cans. Sometimes pecking at a bit of mash or scratching for bugs around the water dispenser. They love to scratch, and they have powerful legs. If you've ever seen or done the dance called "the funky chicken" you can easily visualize the movement. It is no-nonsense, serious, and has a rhythm. I love the way our dances used to imitate the creatures we were obviously fascinated by: chickens, dogs, fish, and of course a long time ago, jitterbugs, among others. Jitterbugs must have been thrilling to watch! Scratching with an intense authority that I find wonderful—chickens' eyes are so sharp they see dozens of edible critters where I see none at all. And gobble them up.

They like to sit on my arm. But they have no sense of what their hard feet and claws feel like; consequently, I've received more than a few scratches. What happens is they're comfy for a moment, maybe two, but then they see a bug, way off at the other end of the yard, and they're off, launched from my arm without any kind of good-bye. I had never understood well enough the use of the gauntlets that falconers wear. But until I can find a pair I will endeavor to wear denim sleeves. But what would throwing down the gauntlet mean, in this context, I wonder?

They like to eat and their favorite thing may be fresh corn, which I give them chilled and on the cob. I tell them it's chicken popsicle. But they also like grapes. And they especially like Chardonnay grapes, much more than Pinot Noir. I so agree with them. There's no comparison, really. Where we live the landscape is over-run with vineyards, with every kind of grape imaginable, but overwhelmingly Chardonnay and Pinot Noir. Thirty years ago when I moved to this valley there were three small vineyards and many pastures full of sheep. I miss the sheep and the pastures. My land is deliberately under-graped. The chickens and I make do with three grapevines, two of Chardonnay and one Pinot Noir. I pick the grapes, smell and admire them, and fling them through the fence, eating a few before doing so. They also love pears and apples, collards and kale, lettuce and eggplant, but not figs. Here we disagree. I *love* figs. They remind me of my father, who, with his rich color and slow-to-ripen sweetness resembled a fig himself. Soon there will be persimmons. I'm excited but a bit edgy. They may not like them. But how could they not like persimmons? Persimmons are orange, a fabulous color. I *love* persimmons. *The mushier the better.* They are the American mango. And how about the pumpkin left over from Halloween?

5

PERHAPS YOU'VE SEEN HER?

PERHAPS YOU'VE SEEN her? A photograph of her, maybe
on a We'Moon calendar? She is an old woman, round,
comfy, wearing a dark-colored headscarf—so maybe
she's in Turkey, or Egypt or Pakistan, Afghanistan or
Iraq—sitting under a tree, or maybe she's on a bench
that's against a wall. Outside anyway and she's gazing
in complete peace at a flock of geese in front of her.
They have those long, dark, graceful necks that one
could, really, stare at for days. Just at the necks and
the beaks and the feathers—best not to wonder about

their livers. But there she is, and peace is with her. How is this? That is the mystery I have fallen into with my/our chickens. I sit in the corner of the chicken yard on my little green stool, Babe in my lap, Gertrude S. in my lap, and I'm there. Eternity. How long have humans and nonhumans been carrying on this way?

I think of being taught formal meditation. It was in New York City and there was a lot of traffic and a lot of horns blowing. Constantly. To duck into one's own "eternity" seemed impossible. It turned out, it wasn't at all. But one thing our teacher stressed was that we must shut any animals out of the room while we sat. I did this. My cat, Tuscaloosa, used to being near me, had to entertain himself at least twice a day for up to half an hour. Whenever he did manage—while I was meditating—to get out of the kitchen where I'd sequestered him and leap into my lap, it was a shock. I thought I understood.

But now, sitting with chickens, I begin to wonder. It feels so natural. It is like another recent discovery I've made with Surprise, my present cat, and Miles, my companion's dog. Surprise, unlike Tuscaloosa ("black warrior," in Choctaw) is an escape artist from any confinement, and she will find me wherever I have secluded myself. Having found me, quietly meditating on cushion or bed, she will not rest until she is in my lap. She will remain there, perfectly still, until meditation is over. It appears to me that she is meditating too. But who knows anything at all about cats? Miles will lie nearby, in complete silence, until I open my eyes or stretch or make some other movement or sound. Then he will stretch, do a couple of downward dogs, and yawn also. Done.

6

I HAVE A PERSISTENT THOUGHT
ABOUT MY MOTHER'S THUMB

IT IS JUST her thumb. I recognize it because I loved it
so well, along with all the rest of her. But the reason
I see it now is because of the chickens. She ordered
them from a catalog; the postman delivered them to
our mailbox at the side of the road, way in the middle
of Beautiful Countryside, Georgia, and she carried the
brown cardboard box carefully down the hill to our
house. It is in the moment of her opening the box that
I notice her thumb. There is a deep scar on it, where
she almost severed half of it with the butcher knife.

Sometimes, looking at the block of knives I use in my kitchen I am wryly amused: there is a knife for boning meat, a knife for paring fruit, a knife for chopping vegetables, a knife for slicing bread. There are knives I never use except to open jars. Who knows what they're really for. But in our house, when I was a child, there was only one knife, the butcher knife, a ten-inch blade screwed into a chunky brown wood handle, and it was used for everything. So she may have nearly sliced her thumb off while cutting a hard cured ham that swung in the smokehouse, or cutting kindling for starting the kitchen fire, or cutting a rope for tethering the cow. But cut it to the bone she did. And then, because there was no doctor, and because she was learned in the ways of folk medicine, she put her two pieces of flesh together again using clay from the dirt daubers that built their nests under the eaves of our house, soot from the chimney, and spider's web. Having applied these medicinals, she wrapped her bleeding thumb—which she had washed as well as she could in cold water from the spring—in a clean cloth, and gone on about her work.

What I see is the tenderness with which she lifts the lid of the box, already having rigged up a low-wattage light bulb (we have recently acquired electricity) for heat, and how she kneels there, with the warm light bulb just where the sun would be, as the two dozen yellow chicks, with their bright orange beaks, fumble and stumble over each other, their just-born faces gradually adjusting to the fresh air, the warmth, and the light. She's not a talker, my mother, but she offers a few encouraging words of welcome, praise, concern. *Did all of you make it? How many lost on the journey? Let's move them out. How hungry are we?*

She will raise these chickens, as well as chickens we have from hens and roosters already established in our yard, and with their help—their eggs and their flesh—she will feed her family of ten.

And something else will happen between my mother and her flock. I see this, now that I am old enough to see her so much better: she will sit with them when we are at school or at church and endless work has prevented her from leaving home, and she will enter the peace that I have found with Babe and Gertrude, & Co., that elusive "eternity"—for someone so busy as she—which meditation has always been.

7

SO I THOUGHT WE WOULD JUST
GO ON LIKE THIS FOREVER

SO I THOUGHT we would just go on like this forever, happy, drowsy, eating grapes; but no. Guess who had to go and enter the picture?

Death.

I was not prepared. Are we ever?

It is painful even to think about.

I had come down the hill in all my cheerful innocence, expecting everything to be the same as it had been the day before. (*Good Morning, Girls, it's Mommy!*) Impossible, of course, but there are many days when we don't think about "impermanence" or how "Everything must change," a phrase I always hear in Nina Simone's voice. Like the child that I still am I count my chickens every time I see them; and that is what I started to do. Feeling almost instantly that somebody was missing. Sure enough, no matter how many times I counted, trying to reach nine, I only got to eight. Eight. Where was chicken number nine? My heart was in my mouth. This is an expression I never hear these days, and I certainly don't hear myself saying it. Still, there it was. I knew something awful had happened.

The flock, by now, seemed over whatever the shock had been and were most curious about what I had brought them. Today, sunflower seeds, with big yellowing petals still attached to the circle of seeds. They didn't know what to make of this at first, but one or two pecks and behold, out popped big crunchy seeds, which, from their perspective, might have been hiding, so cleverly does the flower protect its seeds from the eyes of birds.

I went inside their house, looking at everything carefully: their nests, the roosts, the floor. Way at the back of the coop I saw her: her black and gold feathers, the flecks of orange on her wings. It was Babe. I tried to pick her up but couldn't. Her head was wedged between the outside chicken door and the floor. Someone, closing the door while she was trying to look out or get out, closed the door on her lovely head. I went outside, opened that door, and lifted her body out into the sunlight. There was a lot of blood, now dried, some of it running down the side of the chicken house.

She was heavy. In her few weeks with me she had gained weight. But there was also, on my part, an instant understanding of the expression "dead weight" for she was not just heavy but leaden. The buoyancy of life had left her entirely. And she was stiff and hard. Her feathers the only thing still shining and seeming to have life. Her poor head was crushed, but the rest of her was intact.

What to do?

I took her in my arms and expressed my sorrow. *I am so sorry*, I said. *You met such a frightful fate and I was not here with you. I hope it was quick and painless; that you did not suffer.* I looked for a place to bury her. It happened that I was having a new septic system installed for the guest cottage—a tiny wooden teepee-like dwelling I lived in before building my house. There was a deep hole waiting to be filled, piles of clean earth all around it. I knew I had to place her deep to keep the bobcats, raccoons, and coyotes from finding her and so chose this spot. I dug a deeper small hole inside the larger one and laid her there, covering her gently with prayers for her journey. Who knew this would hurt so much?

And it isn't as if I'm vegan. I'm just an ordinary run-of-the-mill mostly vegetarian person who still eats chicken soup when I'm sick and roast chicken when I can't resist. But I could not have eaten Babe. Though a neighbor, like many folks in this part of the country, thinks he could have, and that not to eat her was in some sense a waste. I don't agree. Nothing good that goes into the earth is wasted, is my thought. Look what magical things come out of it! I have never understood why people choose to be buried so that they don't touch the earth. It seems shortsighted.

I limped back to my stool in the corner of the chicken yard. I blamed myself. For isn't this what mothers do? The day before, following a book on chicken raising, I had done something that might have caused Babe to rush to the chicken door that leads outside, rather than to the door, always open, that leads into the yard. According to my book, I was supposed to keep the chickens in the chicken house and yard for at least two weeks, without letting them out into the garden or the unfenced space around their house. This was to make sure they knew where they lived, and could return there, and to keep them from straying off into the woods, which they would do, since chickens are known to follow any bug anywhere, completely forgetting where they live and are loved or who is waiting impatiently there. I did this. The day before Babe's death the two-week period ended and I happily opened the never-before-opened door to the wide world outside their chicken yard and, with cracked corn and human clucks, showed them how to descend a ladder that extended from that door. They were excited to be free. Who wouldn't be?

Together we went over to an arbor covered by grapevines and wisteria. Wisteria getting the upper hand. In the shade. And, bugs without number, just beneath the moist wood-chip-covered ground beneath the canopy. The chickens were in Paradise. I was too. There's a nice wooden bench to sit on and I sat watching them enjoy their freedom. Overjoyed as they were, they occasionally, Babe and Gertrude Stein especially, came over and hopped up on my lap or shoulder, just to thank me, I guess. We stayed out for an hour, which seemed long enough, and then I coaxed them back to their house with corn and more clucks. They were reluctant to leave but came willingly enough when I threw in a few grapes. Rufus and Agnes of God tried to hide around the other side of the chicken house, but of course I could still see them. Which they didn't seem to believe.

Before leaving the chickens I sat for a quarter hour holding Babe, her resplendent black and gold neck in the crook of my arm, the festively feathered rest of her snuggled comfortably in my lap. *This may be the last time, this may be the last time, this may be the last time, it may be the last time, I don't know.* This old song that my parents and grandparents sang in church came back to me. It was a sad song, melancholy to a child, and even though we attended a funeral almost every month, sometimes twice a month, I was too young to understand the deep compassionate sorrow in their voices. They were people who had been through a lot together, and, because of poverty, the young people were leaving the countryside to go north, or to live in the cities. The community they'd built was coming apart. There was as well much sickness and disease. And some of the old people died after long, mostly invisible to the world lives of sacrifice and hard work. Yet, in this song, they were honored in the singing of people who knew them, appreciated and loved them. *This may be the last time, it may be the last time, I don't know.*

Maybe when a human came and mistakenly opened the outside door she'd come through for the first time only the day before, Babe had rushed toward the light. Perhaps she dreamed of more bugs and cracked corn and grapes, more snuggles in the arms of a warm, soothingly breathing human. Maybe the door closed on her head so quickly she had no time to think of anything else. I hope this was the case. She'd probably never experienced a headache, so maybe she didn't experience her pain as "pain."

On one of his tapes, my teacher Jack Kornfield talks about what we are likely to think about as we're dying. The most important question we will ask ourselves—having long given up asking such questions of others—is "Did I love well?" After all, we're the only ones who could know. I think an acceptable answer is: I loved as well as I could.

What helps me with Babe's death is that the day before, not knowing the future, I sat with her on my lap, stroking and admiring her. It delighted me that her experience of being a chicken on Earth among humans was a loving one. That she ate only the best food, slept in a clean chicken house, had a nest ready for her and her eggs, should she ever happen to lay any. If someone had tried to tell Babe about the cruelty done to chickens by humans, and she could understand the language, she would not have believed them. Her experience, until a human accidentally closed the door to the outside world on her head, was that we are OK. Decent creatures to have in the service of chickens. For that, too, is how she had experienced humans.

8

THANK YOU, RUFUS!

I MUST ONCE again interrupt the strict chronology of these tales to report a thrilling event. It has to do with Rufus, black-and-white Barred Rock Extraordinaire, otherwise known as Juancho. Juancho (rhymes with Pancho) is the name given Rufus by my small friends, J. and K. When their mother told me about it, I had to laugh. What they identified in Juancho and I identified in Rufus was the same quality of rooster-ism. Juancho/Rufus is always the first to greet any visitor to the chicken yard, the first to fluff out increasingly wide shoulders and wings, the first to peck at one's hands, if one is suspected of carrying something to eat, the first to peck at one's knees for some reason I have yet to discern. It's Rufus who has jumped up at me when I've made a startling appearance behind a bundle of straw. And Rufus who has nipped my fingers repeatedly when I've offered cracked corn. I now wear gloves, when I can find them. It is Rufus who stands guard at the chicken-sized door, eyeing any intruder relentlessly. Rufus and Agnes lost their "brother" Bobbie to a bobcat; s/he was every bit as wary and contentious as they. *More about this later.* Many times I have needed to use a stern voice and manner with Rufus and Agnes: they are such firm believers in enforcing the pecking order they constantly terrorize the other chickens. Roosters they are, surely.

And yet.

Coming home recently from a trip to the Far East: Atlanta and New York; I went immediately to visit the girls and Rufus and Agnes. I brought pears. Entering the yard I was once again charmed by their unique sound. The *queraling*, but also something that I resonated with: *Awwwh, hohohohoho*. This was something I could learn rapidly and we could join in a chorus of together, which we did.

As usual I started by counting everybody. There

are now twelve chickens. I counted eleven. Where was the other chicken? With a feeling of suspense, I opened the People door and went inside. There sat Rufus in a nest. *Rufus*, I said, *what's up? Are you sitting in there to keep warm?* It had been and was still quite cold. Rufus paid me no mind. I went about my tasks of scraping poop and turning over straw. I began collecting eggs. Eight eggs, one of them palest green! So the Ameraucanas are beginning to kick in, I thought, gleefully. But also pondering a visit to my eldest brother's house while in the Far East of Georgia. He'd had guests, three white women who, in the Georgia of his youth, would never have been friends with him and his wife and never would have visited him politely in his home and never called him Mr. Fred. We started talking about: yes, chickens. One of them had Ameraucanas. I was too interested. Only her husband refused to eat the green eggs. We had a few rounds of what can be done about such husbands. But more importantly, what can be done about green (and blue) eggs? We both loved the very idea of it, we said, taking a wonderful Sisterhood Is Powerful sort of stance.

So while I was admiring the green egg, Rufus gave a smart cackle and rose from the nest. Expecting nothing but the white massage ball I'd purchased from my chiropractor as a fake egg to encourage laying in the nest, I was shocked to see a brown egg. I reached over and picked it up. Still warm. Rufus!

Rufus, I said, going to the door, *Thank you! What an amazing spirit you are. So strong and aggressive. A bit pushy, "protective," and dominating of the flock . . . and you lay eggs too.*

Paying me no attention whatsoever, Rufus went over to where Gertrude Stein and Babe II were pecking at half a pear. Fiercely pecking Gertrude S. until she fled and kicking at Babe II until she shrieked, Rufus squatted over the pear, which was soon gobbled to the core. Turning about inside the chicken house I noted Agnes of God settling in the same nest Rufus vacated. Sure enough, within a few minutes, while I discreetly found chores to do outside, this "rooster" also laid a warm brown egg. Looking incredibly capable, she descended from the nest and joined Rufus in his pecking and butting and scratching of the other chickens. I broke this up, of course, took down my green stool from its place in the rafters of the chicken house, sat down on it, and gave them a good talking to about their insensitive and deeply regrettable behavior.

They ignored me and instead went to look in the nest from which I'd taken their eggs. They did not seem at all amused that they were gone.

9

DEAR RUFUS, AGNES, & CO.

I HAVE TAKEN a plane that has thus far flown me high over the hills where you (and I) live, on my way to a distant country, India, where I am told there are perhaps more goats—especially in the South—than chickens. I can't imagine it. It was hard to leave you, and I will be gone for quite some time, in chicken terms, but at least before I left I was able to conduct the experiment with persimmons I had long envisioned. The morning I left, I took a few of the ripe and ripening persimmons from the windowsill where I'd placed them—

a wonderful and visually satisfying display of colors I love: deep orange, red, and yellow—and carried them down to you. You were interested, as you always are, in new food and crowded round with the others to see and taste what I had brought. Flinging them toward the far end of your yard, it was gratifying how quickly you were on them, eating away. Like me, you gravitated toward the mushy, very ripe ones, pecking with gusto. But you also seemed curious about the less ripe ones, and even the ones that might be a bit tart. There was an expression that described that tartness when I was a child: it made one's jaws run up. Remembering this, of course I wondered whether chickens have jaws, as such, and whether, with sufficient tartness in whatever you're eating, your jaws also "run up."

Watching you eat the persimmons brought back to me my own early experience of persimmons when I was a child and the tree grew wild in the quietly rolling countryside of rural Outback, Georgia. My siblings loved me, but they could not resist experimenting with my gullible nature. Which I still have, I'm too often told. I liked them so unequivocally; I believed almost anything they told me. So of course they took me to a fruiting persimmon tree the moment I said I wanted to see it, and I was enchanted because it looked like a Christmas tree strung with bright orange balls. They lifted me up to pick a persimmon. They had picked persimmons weeks before and permitted them to ripen near a window in our kitchen. These had been sweet and delicious and had thoroughly awakened my desire for more. With a straight face, my brothers held me patiently on their shoulders as I tugged at the persimmons, eventually detaching a number of them. My desire (an early gluttony for beauty and experience, as I see it now) was fairly intense.

I gave no thought to the fact that the persimmons I'd picked seemed hard, and, as soon as my feet touched the ground, I pushed myself free of my brothers' support and bit into the softest one. It was this moment for which they'd waited. It was worse than biting into a lemon. So tart I thought my jaws would never stop running up. In fact, they seemed to run all the way up to and past my ears. *Space Nut.* Everyone, even my parents, when told about it later, thought this very funny. I found it fairly hard to bear, however, and could only be mollified by the gift of a perfectly ripe persimmon that my oldest brother, F., pulled out of his hat.

I wonder if you will miss me? I already miss you. Even though I am leaving you in very good hands, a number of them. You will have E. and L. and J. and K. and you will also have the dogs, M. and T. Will you even notice that I've gone? I suspect it will be mostly my voice you'll miss, with its accompaniment of leafy greens, seeds, and fruit.

This makes me wonder what it is you see when you look at us. Humans think we look like "somebody." But to a chicken, I doubt we look like anybody at all. From observing you, I'd say that next to your extraordinary interest in whatever we might be carrying in our hands for you to eat, you relate mostly to our eyes. You notice eyes because they shine. Well, you will have twelve shining eyes watching over you. In fact, shininess seems to be what most attracts you. A belt or shoe buckle, an earring, a bracelet or necklace. A fly's wing. It was my sweetheart who warned me to always wear glasses while sitting with you: *They will peck at anything shiny*, I was told. Over time, I saw this was true. That whenever you go after a bug, no matter how small, it is the tiny bit of shine of its skin or carapace that draws you. Cracked corn likewise has luster. Even your mash must appear to your eyes to be sprinkled with gold dust. I hope it is tasty. As tasty as the persimmons that, tart or sweet, have now delivered a previously unknown thrill to your tiny jaws.

10

FLYING

DID YOU EVER really fly? Like birds fly? I've been thinking about this for some time. Especially since the hour,
one late afternoon a few weeks ago, that M. the dog
and I spent watching the birds, at least a thousand of
them, swoop down from the sky to glean in the vineyard we see from our hillside. We had been down to
visit you, and then up to my studio to practice a new
song I'm learning to play on piano—all the songs I'm
learning to play are *very* simple, no more complicated
than your *Awwwh hohohohohoho*—and then we started

home. *M.*, I said, *what is that sound? Is it thunder, is it rain* (though there were no raindrops where we were), *is it wind? Whatever could it be? And look over there, those trees are swaying, one of them in particular.* M. followed my line of questioning with a look of inquiry of his own. Bearing our curiosity, and a basket of produce from the garden, we slogged up the hill. And then I noticed the sky changing and a sound like rain and wind both, and birds without number appeared making a beautiful curve of darkness over our neighbor's vineyard, all scarlet, maroon, claret, and gold in the fading light, picked bare of grapes I had thought, the week before. But apparently not. Landing with chirps of discovery and joy, the birds found grapes and insects on which to feast, and having swept the vineyard once, they all flew over to the same gigantic fir tree a field away from the vineyard and disappeared into its branches. The tree swayed for several minutes under their weight but then became perfectly still. Completely quiet. M. and I were mesmerized. Anticipating even more drama, which Nature unobtrusively observed is so good at exposing, we sat down on the side of the trail and waited.

The birds left the fir tree several times to sweep the vineyard. Then, as the light faded completely, they settled in the tree perhaps to spend the night, and M.

and I, released from the gift of this unexpected experience of Nature still functioning spellbindingly in its numbers, made our way home.

Did you ever fly wild like that? Were there once swooping waves of chickens descending from the sky? Did you ever know such freedom? Did you also once upon a time know when the season was ripe (so to speak) for you to fly south, then north, then south again? Did every cell in your body know when each food source on your path was ready for your visitation and consumption? Or were you domesticated so long ago that this isn't even a memory?

I'm sure humans domesticated you very early because they discovered (perhaps after a forest fire) that cooked, you are delicious, and that uncooked, safe and happy, you produce eggs. No doubt you were enticed into captivity by being offered items of food. Or shelter. This happens to many of us. No doubt humans learned early to clip your wings. And did humans also eventually breed you to eat a lot, to be heavy, so you could not fly high or far? Hmmm . . .

And what is in your brain? What is your mind like? Has it been changed completely? Some humans think highly of big brains. They have done much damage to other creatures because they think their own big brain is of major importance and any being with a smaller brain is somehow deficient. I've never believed this. For instance, your head is small and your brain as well. Yet they both seem adequate for what you appear these days to enjoy most in life. Being with your friends, eating well, sleeping when you want to, enforcing or enduring the pecking order when you feel like it, and making sounds that seem to this human to indicate, at the very least, a sense of integrity of being, contentment, and even, stretching it perhaps, a bit of (chicken) humor.

11
GIRLS!

WE HAD BEEN in India, in the state of Kerala, for almost four days. During that time, I had not seen a single chicken. Driving for two hours in order to take a boat through the backwaters of the state I almost despaired. Not a single chicken in all that time. What could be the meaning of this? It is true we saw three elephants, all in chains. This was very hard to bear. At one stop by the side of the road where a man was working with "his" elephant, we were invited to come close. I went up to the elephant, very old, very present, as elephants tend to be, and very patient. As they also have to be. I placed my hand on his side, and it seemed to me I felt his entire being. Pulsing, throbbing, roiling with life, with thoughts, with emotions. It almost undid me, to tell you the truth. How could such a majestic being still be led about in chains, by a smiling human who asked for a donation? On the other hand, there's widespread malnutrition in India, *hunger*, particularly among children, as there is in many parts of the world. Perhaps this "smiling" man is trying to feed his family. There were more elephants along the way and we bowed to them. But not one chicken. Where were they, we wondered?

Could it be they are all rounded up somewhere and raised as chickens are raised in America? In cages, without sufficient space or light? Fed abominable food and given drugs to make them grow faster than they are intended? Were they in coops behind each house? These were my wonderments.

On the boat, as we cruised waters that have looked the same for thousands of years, we were glad to encounter ducks, hundreds of them, at many turns in the river and along the edges of the spectacular lakes. These were fat and sleek, happily chomping on water hyacinths that threaten to take over the heavily boat-traveled waterways. In fact, seeing the water hyacinth everywhere, even in the town of Cochin, which is also threaded with waterways, I thought of you. Would you like the taste of this plant? Would it be good for you? Should I try to sneak a bit of it back in my bags for you to taste? Would immigration nab me for bringing it in? Etc. Once my sweetheart smuggled fresh collard greens to me in Mexico, but it was a harrowing adventure we would not like to repeat!

I fell asleep thinking of the absence of your kin and woke also with this on my mind.

And then, this morning, just as I was thinking of writing to you, I looked across from where our boat had moored for the night and there they were, your Indian cousins! First, I saw a father, a rooster, black with a red comb; then a mother, grayish and serious, with many tiny chicks. Then I began to see the rest of the community. They were all scratching away under the coconut trees and running along the edges of the raised paths that neatly separate the canals, lakes, and rivers from the rice paddies that stretch into the horizon.

And so I write to you this morning with a light heart. There are free chickens here, as there are also free chickens in Hawaii, where I would so like to take you! But perhaps no free elephants. Which reminds me of what I think you'd like about elephants. You'd like their feet and how so much edible stuff appears to gather in the crevices between cuticles and toenails.

With love,

Mommy

P.S. More good news! According to a new friend who grew up in southern India,[*] there are indeed free elephants, in the jungles, still roaming about in herds; there are also "rogue" elephants that terrorize the humans who try to enslave them. Perhaps fate will deliver a meeting or at least a viewing of these militants before I return home.

----

[*] Arundhati Roy

12

HOW MANY LOST ON THE JOURNEY?

LOSING BABE WAS hard. Losing Bobbie, whose personality was so different, was as bad. It happened this way: a filmmaker came with a crew of four to begin a documentary about my life. I had almost forgotten I'd made this commitment. There we were, the girls and me, maybe one or two roosters, guys (we thought), all immersed in the bliss of high summer. Long days golden to the bone, plenty of food dropping off every vine and bush, fish jumping and cotton high . . . you get the picture. We had begun to establish a routine.

Each afternoon around four o'clock, as the day was beginning to cool, I let the chickens out of their house and yard through the magic door to the outside world, and herded them over to the arbor and a daily feast of insects. I even used something that resembled a shepherd's crook, a tall Huichol walking stick with a deer, the most revered of symbols among the Huicholes, carved at one end.

Of course I thought of Babe. How could I not? Her dried and fading blood was still on the side of the chicken house; I should have scrubbed it off, but I didn't, which I later realized was one reason predators increased their visits. What I did instead was more typical of my kind of mind (that of a believer in art, shamanism, and interspecies magic). I hurried down to our local African store; thank goodness one exists on our coast, and there bought a beautiful dreadlocked Haitian angel, hammered out of a metal drum, to nail over the ill-fated door that had closed on Babe's head. This angel's crown and halo is her hair, and at her feet are birds and in her hands are birds, and she is setting one or more of them free. In her role as angel, she is both protector and liberator. In Western thought her presence over the place where Babe died would represent a tombstone; in my thought she represents blessings, loving memory, sorrow. And, as well, a desire to be more mindful. To do better. Though as we shall see, doing better was not immediately implemented.

All along I had been aware of, distracted by, something new happening with the chickens: they followed the sound of my voice. Lovely! I adored this and enjoyed the way they looked as they scratched and explored fresh terrain in their newly acquired freedom. Is there anything more captivating than the complete self-absorption of insect-hunting chickens? I don't think so. It was getting late, the sun about to go down. Chickens look for their roosts as soon as they lose the sun. It should be easy for the film crew to drop bits of corn in front of them and thereby lead them down the hill. So I thought.

In the middle of the night, though, I woke abruptly from a deep sleep. I could feel something was wrong. Grabbing boots and flashlight and jumping into the "whoopdi," a vehicle I use to drive down the hill at night, I went to check on the chickens. I entered their house and carefully counted them as they slept soundly on their roosting posts. I was one short. I went round and round outside the chicken yard looking for whoever was missing. There was not a movement, not a sound.

Next morning, early, I came down to see what I could do. I discovered it was Bobbie, a member of the Barred Rock Trio that was missing. She/He had a habit of running past the ladder that led back into the chicken house and getting stuck in a corner outside the yard. This was amusing to me; it made me laugh to watch her misunderstanding of the nature of corners, being backed into or stuck in one. A corner is always temporary; it can be backed out of! Humans forget this also and flail away fruitlessly whenever they find themselves stuck. It is better to sit still, maybe take a nap, right there in the offending "corner" and see what comes to one. Like magic, after a rest, all corners develop windows! Passageways, doors! Besides, there's always the space directly over one's head that is hopefully (many believe) inhabited by one's Higher Power. Perhaps Bobbie would have learned this, had she lived.

I looked everywhere. Having no success, I decided, though it was morning, to let the chickens out again, before the film crew woke up. This I did. However, as they happily ran over to their favorite insect-hunting area beneath the arbor, and I turned to close the garden gate, I heard a loud squawk and turned just in time to see a figure, as big as a dog, dark gray, already in the midst of the chickens. I ran to their defense and the creature disappeared into the woods. In less than a flash, it was gone. The chickens were so disturbed, however, it was easy to talk them back to the shelter of their home.

I searched the area again and near the corner of the chicken house where Bobbie used to get stuck, I saw a tiny nest of feathers. Not even enough feathers to notice, unless you were really looking. The predator, whatever it was, had more or less inhaled Bobbie. I wondered if Bobbie had made the sound that, though I did not remember it, had awakened me from sleep.

I went to the Internet. There I learned of the many creatures, other than humans, that like to eat chickens. Foxes, raccoons, snakes, rats, bobcats, mountain lions, hawks, gophers, and coyotes, maybe even voles and moles.

I blamed my exhaustion for not seeing the flock home safely, myself. And the vanity it requires to help create a documentary about one's self. The hardest part was watching Gertrude Stein day after day wait for, and look for, Bobbie, who had been her special friend. They had napped side by side in the heat of the day, their bodies half-buried in dirt and straw. They had hunted insects together under the wood chips in the garden; they had roosted side by side each night on the roosting post. Gertrude's face was wistful, sad, waiting. I wondered if she had witnessed Bobbie's disappearance; if so, it must have shocked and frightened her. I wondered if she was still pondering "death," as she had seen it, the unexpected nature of this encounter we must all experience, the incredible mystery.

I took her on my lap and talked to her the way the old people talked to children who lost loved ones when I was little. I was astounded to hear myself talking about Bobbie being up in heaven, with angels playing on harps and sitting on golden settees. I don't believe in a heaven other than Earth. Still, since these were all chicken angels and the golden settees resembled nests of straw, and Gertrude Stein seemed to like the story, I, like the old people of my youth, went on and on with it, embellishing as I went.

13

GANDHI SAMADHI

The elephant makes a gurgling sound, from the throat, on seeing his favorite mahout or owner. Similarly it may excrete dung or urinate, to express its happiness. All these are considered as good signs.

—Wikipedia

SO, GIRLS, WE went today to pay our respects to a man who never ate a single chicken!* Mahatma Gandhi. Like you, he ate only plants and grains. There is a beautiful garden surrounding the place where he was cremated. Cremation is a notion of which you are innocent, and I will not attempt to explain. And, as we were getting out of the car, guess what we saw? A big neat pile of fresh elephant dung! Right there, in front of the Samadhi entrance, in front of our feet. It was too thrilling! Of course I thought of you. It was in huge yellow balls, and I wondered about the kind of grass that bright color represented, or whether the elephant had been eating his or her lei of marigolds? Sometimes elephants are decked out beautifully with many flowers. Still chained, though. In any case, it looked like something you would spend hours scratching and pecking in. And I knew, even before I checked with Wikipedia, that this was a good sign, a message

---

* I was mistaken about this: rereading Gandhi's autobiography after many decades I rediscovered he did have two periods in his life when he was a meat-eater, which particularly distressed his mother. This autobiography, *The Story of My Experiments with Truth*, is invaluable for many reasons, not the least of which is Gandhi's candid assessment of child marriage: he and his bride were both thirteen. He offers insight also into how, in a patriarchal society, out-of-control feelings of sexuality can lead to tyranny over one's female spouse. How Gandhi treated his wife, Kasturba, as a young man, was one of the great regrets of his life.

from "the Gods" of Earth: elephants and chickens and trees and so forth, that all was in divine order on this and all travels.

I also read this:

If the elephant remains motionless (without flapping its ears), when approached, then one must be wary of it. (The elephant I'd touched had flapped its ears—I sighed with relief.)

Also: in Malayalam (the language of Kerala) elephants are called *kanveeran*, meaning "the black hero." So there!

All my love,
Mommy

14

MOMMY IS NOT PURE!

DEAR GIRLS,

Mommy is missing you terribly, even while she is having a wonderful adventure—so many new ideas to digest, so much good food to enjoy. In India it is easy to be a vegetarian because the Hindus who live here don't eat meat. Some of them do, I guess, along with meat-eating Muslims, but there is a tradition of non-harming and non-meat-eating among them, which makes a Hindu person pretty safe for chickens. Though some of them are quite violent against other humans.

Alas! Which reminds me of your aunt Pratibha, Hindu born, when she came to visit and make her film. She said to me as I was extolling your virtues: *Do you still eat chickens?* And I said to her, truthfully: *Yes, about ten of them a year, some years; other years I might eat none; but I brush my teeth and gargle before coming down to hang out with mine.* She laughed, but I have felt the seriousness of the question. So on this pilgrimage, as I've visited Gandhi's cremation site, and then the place where he was martyred, and while I was led around the grounds by his granddaughter, Tara, whom I liked instantly, the way I liked you when we first met, I've determined not to eat the flesh of any creature, and certainly not chicken. I managed pretty well, because in addition to having this intention, I found I was drawn to the delicious variety of vegetable daals and curries that are the foundation of classic Indian cuisine.

Once, on a plane from Delhi to Bangalore, the flight attendant handed me a chicken curry by mistake and I bit into it. I ate a tiny sliver and could go no further. The only other time was at a dinner in our honor in Dharamsala with the political leader of Tibet in Exile, Professor Rinpoche. Tibetans don't seem as dedicated to vegetarianism as Hindus, perhaps because in the Himalayas, which have a short growing season for grains, animals are traditionally raised for human sustenance, as they were in my childhood and as they are in many areas of the world. I bit into a gravy-covered piece of chicken that I thought was a mushroom but recovered myself quickly and left the uneaten portion on my plate. It is my hope that this piece of uneaten chicken did not go to waste, after the sacrifice of the chicken's life, but that some dog—of which we've seen many in Dharamsala—would be the beneficiary.

We spent part of Christmas Day with a human much loved by many, His Holiness the Dalai Lama. I don't know if he eats chicken, but as a boy his family ate pork; he tells a funny story about that, and about how much he enjoyed it. He's very honest and down to earth about things, including eating. I find his attitude, about much of what we might consider our shortcomings, *forgiving*. I don't know what one would have to do to fall completely outside his grace. How relaxing this is! I wanted a blessing on an upcoming attempt to hold a freedom march in Gaza, where 1.5 million humans are confined in a tiny space you would find intolerable, and also to ask his counsel on what the world can do to free Aung San Suu Kyi from the generals in Burma. He laughed as he spoke about the Myanmar (Burmese) generals—that they are so obviously dominated by the Chinese government—and advised working with those Palestinians and Israelis who all along have been working together to bring peace to their land; to strengthen our connection, and offer support and encouragement, to both peoples.

This seemed wise to me and it is the commitment and discipline also of CodePink, the women organizers of the march, as well. If we choose one people over the other, forgetting there are peacemakers in each group, we risk harming people who are really our allies and friends.

But that is not what I wanted to write you about. I wanted to tell you how odd it is to experience Christmas in faraway lands. It is a strange holiday anyway, perhaps the strangest, devoted almost entirely to buying and selling; you would not understand it at all. Probably. Though you might enjoy leftovers from the gigantic dinners that are prepared, if they were still crunchy and not cooked to death. It is a day supposedly celebrated as the birthday of a venerated spiritual teacher, a person I happen to love very much; you would have liked him too, though I'm sure he ate everything, including chicken and the lamb he is sometimes depicted holding, and though he lived quite a long time ago. His name was Jesus, and he was from the same part of the world where we are planning to hold the freedom march; it has been a problem area, with groups of people dominated and treated badly, for some time. To try to connect the people frenetically shopping to the life of this person who grew up to teach tolerance and love, and who never shopped, going by his clothing, the current holy men come out in droves. The main one is called the Pope and he zooms around in something called a Pope Mobile. The few times I saw a television in India, usually while in transit in airports, he was everywhere. In newspapers, too, there were endless pictures of him.

Guess what happened, though? Whenever I looked at an image of the Pope, he turned into One of You! What fun this was! You were dressed as you always are, splendidly, in your iridescent feathers and vibrant red combs; only now you also wore a pointed white cap covered with jewels.

I realized, later, while visiting temples of thousands of Buddhas and lamas and goddesses, all graceful and intense, that as far as I'm concerned, you are missing from this realm. Not one chicken memorialized and worshiped in all these shrines. I don't understand it. With your flesh and eggs, surely holy, you feed the world. Yet no one bows to you. How can this be?

15

THE OLD FOX

ONE OF THE books I would like to read to you is *The I Ching*. I love it for its profound observation of non-human animals. It does a marvelous job of understanding humans, too, of course, but it is remarkable in its grasp of how much we learn from our cousins who study and comprehend us but cannot, in human language, speak. For instance, there is the story of the old fox crossing an ice-covered pond on tiptoe because she knows the ice may break. She is fine until she almost reaches the other side. Then the ice breaks! She almost falls in (which would mean drowning) but instead, because she has been careful, she only gets her tail wet! This is to say that Mommy, having traveled from the most southern part of India, Kerala (very hot), to the most northern part, the foothills of the Himalayas (very cold), had avoided getting sick until the very last day of her visit.

And, My Children, air pollution, a major health hazard in the urban world of humans (the atmosphere to my lungs in New Delhi, and later, Cairo, looked like a thick dust made from your chicken mash) was a big factor also.

But really, what is not amusing in this world, or at least thought provoking, once we stop coughing?

So on the very next to the last day, feeling fine, but tiptoeing across thin ice, high in the foothills of the Himalayas, almost on a lark, I accepted an invitation to consult a doctor of Tibetan medicine about some old health challenges I thought I'd already overcome.

You will be happy to know that Mommy is basically healthy. That is because of our garden, which, with your rich poop, we shall continue into infinity. The most interesting thing he said though was that I must overcome a tendency to impatience. It turns out impatience is the thief of serenity! The moment he said this, I knew it was true, even though I like to think I am the soul of patience: like most humans, I am most patient and serene when I'm alone. But guess what? Dharamsala (the locals say Dharamshala) is one big hill. By the time I'd climbed the hill to the clinic (even though, truthfully, we climbed it in a van) I'd already climbed hundreds of steps and stairs and wandered up a couple of trails. And the air, very thin, and with a needlelike cold embedded in it even in the sun, had hardly seemed sufficient to get me from one level to another. However, Mommy, having walked up so many hills, has a strategy, which is to walk up steep hills on a slant and sideways. The Tibetans who dash up and down their hills with the grace of mountain goats may have been amused at my way with hills. But another time when I return to visit them and they've aged a bit, I'll explain it to them. This way of climbing hills saves the knees.

I meditated on what the Tibetan doctor said about my impatience and realized something to ponder: I am most impatient with people who don't think the way I do. This isn't the same as feeling impatient with people who have different opinions; I like this, for the challenge of it. No, I become impatient with people whose minds seem beamed from a completely different universe. In the world of astrology, one might say: Oh, Cancers and Capricorns. Maybe Librans. But it isn't as simple as that. My mind, I realize more calmly now as I enter late middle age, is the classic monkey mind; it is nonlinear in the most profound way. In short, without training, it is capable of being all over the place. Like a real monkey, it seems to jump from imaginary branch to imaginary branch and then, as if by magic, it lands where the nuts are. Or the fruit.

But this is why Life gives us teachers. And you, My Girls, have been very helpful to Mommy in this regard. Remember when, after Glorious was eaten up by the chicken hawk, and Mommy was withdrawing from you out of fear and sorrow, and we humans thought bringing in more chickens would help us all feel better? Remember that? E. and L. and G. and Mommy had a long (by chicken terms) collaboration: How to do this? Would the "old" chickens get along with the "new" ones? E. thought we should introduce one new chicken at a time. But I thought no. One new chicken probably wouldn't last long, from what I'd been reading in my chicken manual. I thought we should bring in the whole gang of new chickens and, in their numbers, they could duke it out with the gang of chickens already established in the chicken house. Ultimately, this is what we did. We introduced six new chickens at once, the Red Gang of Six.

Oh, the way you treated them! I was heart-sickened. I was appalled. I had only known you as gentle and cuddly, blissed out on Chardonnay grapes and kale leaves. You were vicious to your new mates. You pecked and scratched them; you wouldn't let them near the food and water. You didn't want Mommy to be Mommy to anyone other than you. When I tried to share goodies with the Red Gang of Six you wouldn't allow it, unless I forced you out of the way. I was so embarrassed for you. Were these the "children" I thought I was raising? But guess what? From your point of view, as chickens, you were doing what comes naturally to chickens: you were creating the pecking order that chickens live by.

My impatience with your behavior led to a withdrawal from you. I felt disappointed and deeply saddened. This made me stay away for days (at least two). When I went back to visit, you were still at it. Mean as could be. Abusive and ugly. Yes, ugly. Mommy found this brutalizing behavior so hideous she could hardly look at you. And when you jumped into her lap, wanting a cuddle, sometimes she stood up. It was this event, when she felt she simply could not bear you in your meanness, that was probably the most serious threat to Mommy's health and heart.

That moment of pushing you away—while you looked at Mommy as if she'd lost her mind—was the flowering of impatience.

16

ENOUGH MOTHER

MY DARLING GIRLS,

What is always so energizing about being with you is your curiosity: What's that shiny thing hanging from Mommy's ear? An earring. What's that shiny thing sliding down her nose? Her glasses. What's that shiny thing . . . oh, many of them, going down the front of her blouse. Buttons! What a funny sound they make between the beak. Beaks? Bills? Being a bit winded by the walk down the hill, Mommy retrieved her green stool from the rafters and sat down on it. But she hopped up in less than a minute because she forgot the first thing she wanted to do was see if there were fresh eggs. So, Mommy opened the People door and went inside. She went from nest to nest. Many were empty. But the nests with the chiropractor's balls were swimming in eggs, the bigger chiropractor ball like a white boulder in the middle of an egg ocean. She was too thrilled.

My goodness, she cried. *All these eggs. Everyone must be laying now.* Because, when Mommy left to go abroad (she likes saying "abroad" because it is so old fashioned) only a few of the girls were laying. And that reminds Mommy of one of the things she wanted to write about: how to tell when a hen is laying. Mommy did not know how you knew this, and she would every day collect the eggs and look at them for any resemblance to their parent. Yes, she did that, and Mommy is probably old enough to know better. Whoever heard of an egg looking like the chicken who layed it. But then again, Mommy is a poet. Anyway, she would look at the light-green egg and know it was from one of the Ameraucanas; look at the light-brown eggs . . . and then it got tricky. It could be the Barred Rocks, Rufus and Agnes of God, or it could be, maybe, one of the Red Gang of Six. Mommy was wondering also whether and what to name the gang. It didn't seem quite right to give them a group moniker. Mommy herself is a strict individualist, except when she's prejudiced.

So what happened? Her next knoll over neighbor, Sue Hoya Sellars, the great painter, goat raiser, cheese maker, the best roaster of goat and chicken in the world, came to visit. She and Mommy took a stroll about the garden, picking collards and kale and digging out a few potatoes and onions. Mommy of course wanted to brag about her girls. *Oh*, she said, *they are laying. At least some of them are.*

Do you know which ones? asked Sue, her head cocked and her bright blue eyes giving her an adorable chickenlike countenance.

I don't, said Mommy, somewhat wistfully. She didn't really care, and still it would have been nice to know.

Well, said Sue, *here's how you tell.* Mommy has learned so much from Sue! She waited with joy.

Sue reached down and picked up Rufus. *See her red comb?* she said. Then she put Rufus down and picked up Hortensia. Mommy never writes about Hortensia. But there she was. A striking vision of black and gold, with less orange and more yellow in her neck ruffle.

This one, said Sue. *Hortensia*, said Mommy.
This one isn't laying. See how pale her comb is?

73

Mommy looked closely. It was true. Rufus's comb was fiery red; Hortensia's merely pink.

When they start to lay, said Sue, putting Hortensia back on the ground, *their combs turn. Isn't that the coolest?*

Mommy agreed. It sure was. She was wondering all kinds of things. For instance, in humans, what was the equivalent of the comb? Had hers, whatever it was, turned?

She thought of her friend Jean Shinoda Bolen who had taught her something just as wonderful as what Sue was teaching her. Mommy didn't recall how it happened but somehow she had been in a circle of women who had lost their mothers, hated their mothers, didn't know their mothers, or were estranged from their mothers. Motherless women! And they were all mad because nobody should be without their mother! This was their feeling, even though in truth they might not have liked her at all.

And Jean said: *Now, here's the magical thing about Mother. There's always enough.*

The women looked skeptical and someone snorted and said: *Usually enough is too much.*

But Jean continued because she is a wise woman and relentless teacher: *Here's how it goes*, she said. *We all know the world is full of women who feel motherless, and that is not their fault. However, what most women don't know is this: that if you collect seven women and form a circle together, enough Mother will automatically be created. Ample Mother will appear.*

Well! The women were all over this gift. It meant nobody need ever be motherless!

And so Girls, that is what I hope for you. When Mommy's away, and Mommy's away a lot because Mommy is a nomad, you yourselves, being twelve strong females, can create me in my absence. You can create the Mother you need. It is only Mommy, out flying about the Earth, who cannot create you, except in her thoughts of your sweet, mostly cuddle- and food-interested ways, and the wonder of you which she carries nestled in her heart.

17

LEAVING YOU

ONE DAY, I was stopped at the gate to the chicken house by a strong sense that you wanted me to stay. I stood for a few seconds with one foot raised in the air. What to do? Some of my feelings became a bit scrambled (no pun!) when I was a little girl; members of my family were always leaving home and I did not understand why they wanted to go anywhere, especially if they loved me, as they seemed to. Nobody talked about "loving" anybody in those times. But you could still tell because love is that kind of emotion; where it exists, it's all over the place. Where it doesn't exist humans claim they don't think about it; usually they're untruthful. So Mommy was stoic. They went. She stayed. They waved good-bye, she waved good-bye. They might be gone for half a decade, coming back looking and smelling and behaving entirely differently. She learned to let her heart shrug. Or maybe she put it to sleep. Because in reality, losing all her sisters and brothers in this way hurt a lot. But when you're really little, or even not so little, what do you do with this feeling that nobody names?

So in a way, Mommy, with you, is just waking up. Isn't that funny? And this was one of those times. She stopped, with one foot raised outside the gate to your yard, one foot inside. *Hmmm*, she thought. *I feel really odd. Even a little dizzy.* If her heart had been an egg she would have heard it start to crack.

Mommy noticed Gertrude Stein in particular. Gertrude Stein, unlike her namesake, was always the smallest of the chickens. That is probably why Mommy's young friends, K. and J., became accustomed to holding her in their arms, even before Mommy started doing this. There stood Gertrude Stein just by Mommy's foot. She had the look she'd had after losing Bobbie to the Predator Inhaler. Mommy brought her foot back inside the gate to the chicken house and picked her up. *Oh*, she felt in her heart, *this is what I wish my sisters and brothers had done! Brought that foot back up on the porch, back inside the house. I wish they had picked me up! And not only that, I wish they had stayed home! Or taken me with them! Though how could I have left school? Left our parents? My mother, especially?*

Now, after half a century, of course Mommy understood why they had to go away. Why they, too, had to be stoic. They had to travel far away from home to find work. And sometimes to avoid encounters with people who were dangerous.

With one hand Mommy reached down her stool from the rafters and sat on it, Gertrude Stein nestled contentedly in her lap. Because she was slightly chilled and Gertrude Stein very warm (chickens are super warm-blooded) Mommy placed one hand under a wing, the other under Gertrude's body, covering Gertrude's gray, scaly, entirely precious feet. She looked down into the orange-colored feathers with their Aubrey Beardsley–like designs. *How extraordinary you are*, she murmured. And, stretching out the wing her hand was under: *How beautiful you are too!* She thought of all the children in the world who eat chickens but do not realize this about them: that they are beautiful. This made her sad. It wasn't that she felt no children anywhere should eat chickens; she was a

79

fervent supporter of Heifer International and some-times sent, through them, chickens and other animals to poor families whose survival meant having the oc-casional animal to eat. And she also, on occasion, ate chicken herself. No, she grieved knowing what chil-dren missed when they had no opportunity to learn to appreciate what they were eating. How marvelous it was. Not just its taste in their mouth but in its very Being.

In fact, she could have boo-hooed right there. She had this thought: Maybe after this lifetime some of us do come back as crocodiles. And, previously hu-man, we have learned about the beauty of what we are eating; but as crocodiles, we have to eat flesh to live. Maybe that is why crocodiles cry when they're having lunch; they remember. Mommy thought: and maybe that is why humans cry crocodile tears even before they become crocodiles. There was a part of her that did cry when she was eating something that once was beautiful in its own feathers or scales, darting about eating gecko eggs or krill.

Gertrude Stein did that wonderful thing chickens do when they're cradled and warm: she dropped into a swoon and nodded off with her eyes still open. Then they started to close. Mommy too was very comfort-able, though still a bit chilled; *next time*, she thought,

I'll wear a warmer coat. She also hoped she wouldn't get straw dust or chicken dander in her nose and begin to cough. That would be such a disturbance of the moment! Sitting with Gertrude Stein made Mommy think of Glorious, and how she was lost. And the loss of Glorious would always be connected to the loss of Michael Jackson, whom Mommy always called in her mind: St. Michael.

18

ST. MICHAEL

DEAR GIRLS,

The week that Michael Jackson died, Mommy was in a state of shock. She could do nothing, really, but come sit with you. Or with her human sweetheart, or with the other "children"; the dog, Miles, and the cat, Surprise. Spending time with you was especially comforting, and she sat some part of each day with one or the other of you on her lap. She also became even more obsessed with your freedom. How to protect you from predators and how to keep you safe if indeed you wandered beyond the enclosed confines of your house and yard. What pained her so much about the loss of Michael was the loss of his own innocence, seeing it offered to adoring fans who did not have a clue, many of them, how precious was the gift they were consuming. Because to Mommy, looking at a photo of the young Michael, when he was bursting with love of life and the joy of giving himself to others in song, he was a special being, sent to us for a special reason. It seemed to her almost everyone forgot to keep wanting to know: what was that reason?

Sometime in the midst of grieving, Mommy figured out that she could let you out into the vegetable garden, if not all the way underneath the grape arbor that unfortunately circles into the woods where the big gray predator that steals chickens seems to lurk. She would have to sit with you while you scratched and ate. This is what she did.

Mommy's *Curandera*, who lives on the coast, also raises chickens. Once when she was about to stick an acupuncture needle in Mommy's third eye Mommy told her of her dream to have chickens running about the vegetable garden ridding it of bugs. Her friend laughed. *I don't advise it*, she said. Then she told Mommy of her experience of letting her chickens run free in her garden. *They ate, shredded, scratched up ev-*

erything, she said. *By the time they were through, there was very little left for us to eat that wasn't pecked.* So Mommy had waited. But now, her own love of liberty kept her awake at night, imagining chickens felt the same way about freedom she did. How could she give them freedom and keep them safe?

So there Mommy sat, having opened your gate—through which you poured like a fluffy tide—surrounded by a flock of liberated chickens. You were acting just as my friend said: messing up everything. But by then I didn't care. *Go ahead,* I thought, *mess it up. I will eat the plants with the holes in them. Why not?* And in fact, the more I let go of caring about the damage, the more I relaxed, even exulted, in the freedom you seemed to feel. And then up walked Glorious, who looked me kind of in the eye or maybe she was looking into one of my buttons, and hopped into my lap.

Glorious, of all of you, was the most sensuous; and I know you don't hear that said much about chickens. But she was. Once in a lap she could nestle in and stay as long as possible, until the lap stood up. Then she would lie where she fell, seemingly in a swoon of ecstasy. She would remain in that state for several minutes, until Rufus or Agnes came over and started to peck at imaginary insects underneath her. I named her Glorious for the shining straw-colored grasses of midsummer, when northern California puts on such a show of opulence and ease. Everything golden and still. Warm. Everything growing. Or dying. But quietly.

I had dragged my meditation camping chair that folds out of storage and we were sitting in it together underneath the windmill. I think this was the day of Michael's memorial or perhaps the day after it. What can one do at such times? I think: *Hold something that is alive. Breathe with it. Feel its heart. Offer yours. What else is there?*

However, I remembered I had left a burner on up the hill in the kitchen and decided to put Glorious down and go up to turn it off. I did this. When I returned, she was gone.

Just like that.

I looked everywhere. The garden fence wasn't too tall for a determined predator to scale, but it was unlikely one had done so during the fifteen minutes I had been gone. Of course I thought maybe some hungry human had slipped in and stuck Glorious under his arm. But we are miles from anywhere and there're not that many hungry humans passing our place. And then I remembered my love of hawks, the way they look when they've spotted prey and how they stop just above it in the air and seem to be standing still, though their wings are flapping. Then they drop. This had always excited me before, even though I felt sorry for the mouse, rat, rabbit, snake, or whatever animal was being grabbed and then borne away. It had not occurred to me that this same fate could befall one of my chickens!

And not just any one of you, but Glorious.

And then, in my sadness to lose Michael and Glorious in the same week, I realized there is no reliable protection we can guarantee for another being, as much as we would like to do so. Freedom is a big risk, as is loving. Michael and Glorious are perhaps showing us by their lives and deaths what they came onto the planet to let us know: that each day is to be cherished, each moment of closeness with another deeply appreciated, each memory of innocence treasured, valued, and passed on.

Mommies can't be everywhere. Only Nature can be everywhere.

It has its ways.

19

ST. MICHAEL,
LOVER OF ANIMALS AND CHILDREN

THAT YOU OFFERED
your light
while you were
too young
to comprehend
our darkness:

We promise, St. Michael
to learn from you.

That you were
injured in spirit
while still
a child
& that you
presented your
joy
regardless
of hurt:

We promise, St. Michael
to learn from you.

That you knew
you were love
loving itself
in those you
adored:

We promise, St. Michael
to learn from you.

That exhausted
from over-giving
you lost
the energy

to protect
your gift:

We promise, St. Michael
to learn from you.

That your arrows
were scalpels
turned against
blameless
flesh:

We promise, St. Michael
to learn from you.

That your heart
refused
work
no slave
on the plantation
of fame
could accomplish
in fifty
venues:

We promise, St. Michael

to learn from you.

That you loved
the simple
vulnerable beings
of this earth:
the trees
the children
& the animals:

We promise, St. Michael
to learn from you.

That in your unique
loneliness
you thought
it best
to
erase
yourself:

We promise, St. Michael
to learn from you.

That in your reading
of us

92

in our bondage
you sought
to
offer what
we seemed
to desire:

We promise, St. Michael
to learn from you.

That the Self
is
already
perfect
with no need
to be
redefined:

We promise, St. Michael
to learn
from you.

That to be wealthy
in everything
but freedom
& joy

is to be poor
beyond
bearing:

We promise, St. Michael
to learn from you.

That we are
as we are
splendid
to all who
love us
including
ourselves:

We promise, St. Michael
to learn from you:

&
we thank you.
That you left us
abruptly
to ponder
these things:

We promise, St. Michael

to learn from you.

& by
our learning
of so much truth
that we have avoided
for so long
& to our
decline
may we repay you
—a very small offering—
for your indescribable
even unimaginable
suffering
from which
we may—
awakening
to our own beauty—
benefit.

We promise, St. Michael
to learn from you.

And we thank you.

20

THE SONG BEHIND THE WORLD:
THE NUNS OF DHARAMSALA

GIRLS,

Today Mommy is planting okra in another country. As she presses the soil around the seedlings she is reminded of many things: of you, and how you would eat the seeds and the seedlings, if given the chance, and of my trip to Dharamsala to visit His Holiness the Dalai Lama. The waiting and conversing rooms in the Dalai Lama's palace are very nice and spacious, not fancy, and the palace is on a hill; it is across from a temple with many sculptures of the Buddha. (Mommy thinks it should be called his house and not his palace because "palace" always makes Mommy think of feudalism, a condition to which she has no intention of returning). After a warm and cheerful visit with him, which Mommy and Daddee and our friend Devaki enjoyed very much, we were taken down the hill to visit nuns who live in a very different part of Dharamsala. They live in the flatlands. Mommy was doing her usual thing of thinking: *Oh, why are the women way down here? Hidden from view?* Etc. The road down the hill was a long one, followed by a road to the convent that was fairly rough. But then, just at the end of this road, there stood the most exquisite monastery. Large, spacious, airy, with wonderful slate roofs at different levels, and cherry trees just beginning to bud. Inside, in addition to dormitory space, there was a library and classrooms. From the back windows of the library Mommy leaned into the beauty of lush and ample grounds with gardens, irrigated by what appeared to be a solar-powered water system. Behind all this rose the majestic Himalayas. It was breathtaking. The soul of woman, the spirit of woman, could find peace here. Mommy was sure of it, and so happy to have her cynicism squashed.

Through the beautiful but empty hallways and rooms we went, until we were led to a huge door from behind which came a faint hum. Our guide gently opened this door, which liberated a tidal wave of sound. There before us were hundreds of nuns in dark red and ochre robes, seated at desks on the floor, chanting an ancient prayer. The sound of these nuns praying was like a billion bees buzzing. And best of all, they were not even attempting to pray in unison but were chanting wherever they were on the page, which meant a dissonance that brought life and spontaneity to the words and urgency to the prayer. It was so powerful and unexpected it nearly floored Mommy. In fact, Mommy sat right down among the nuns and let herself be bathed in the sound of what felt like an ocean of prayer. If she could have lain down without offending anyone, she would have. She could have stayed there forever; she never wanted to leave.

She wanted to come back to you, though, even so!

Mommy had this realization: that behind the world, always, there is a song. That behind every country's "leadership" and every country's "citizenry" there is a song. Behind Tibet, behind the spiritual "country" the Dalai Lama and Professor Rinpoche and the Tibetan Government in Exile have formed, there is the song of the nuns, which is the song of the feminine. Without this song there is no movement, no progress. It is this song that keeps it all going, though we may

99

hear it infrequently or only by accident. For millennia and to our detriment, it has been deliberately drowned out. But it is there, nonetheless. Mommy was ecstatic to hear it.

It is the same with you and with the other animals of the planet. You are the song behind the world human animals inhabit. *Awww . . . hohohohohoho . . . .* This is the vocal song you sing as chickens, but each animal has its song in its very being: we are our songs embodied; it is the song of all of us that keeps our planet balanced.

What about extinction of any singer? What about missing, or mangled, notes?

21

SITTING WITH THE ANGELS
WHO HAVE RETURNED
WITH MY MEMORIES

DEAREST GIRLS,

It has taken all this time, decades, for Mommy to begin to comprehend what is going on. Why seeing a chicken and her babies in Bali so long ago struck me, why of all the magical encounters experienced in that astounding land this is the one that has stayed with me. It isn't simply that writers and poets are strange; we are. It is that we are sent, at least it seems so, that which is our need. Mommy's need was to be able to remember part of a childhood that was hidden behind, she thought, a trauma that happened to her. But now she thinks this was not the case; that the trauma that happened to her, though indelible, was not the trauma that robbed her of memory. Now she thinks the trauma was something else, something connected with you. Not, of course, with you as you exist in the present, but as you existed in hidden memory, represented by the chicken and her family that Mommy saw in Bali.

Mommy believes the chicken she saw in Bali led her not only to you but also to her severed memories. That is why, just today, and after writing many chapters of this little book, Mommy realized what the subtitle should be: *Sitting with the Angels Who Have Returned with My Memories*. You are the angels.

For, spending time with you, not only did Mommy recall and visualize her own mother's thumb with its deep, beloved scar, and from the thumb begin to see her mother's face and actions, but she also began to see, in stark detail, the house near Ward's chapel: the final and most wretched of all the gray shacks; the house that her mother attempted to hide, as she camouflaged all the others, behind a vibrant wall of flowers. And inside the house that shook when anyone walked from room to room, there was Mommy's room papered with real wallpaper, though too thin and delicate to actually touch! While in her parents' room her mother had done the Mommy thing that was so typical of her: she had papered her own bedroom with flattened cardboard boxes and brown butcher's paper.

Not only did Mommy begin to remember details of the house, for instance the splintered pine boards with cracked knot holes and bark-covered pointy ends that were rejects from the lumber mill, tacked onto the sagging house frame vertically rather than horizontally; but she also remembered the lush okra patch filled with plants whose stalks were studded with bright yellow blossoms. An okra patch that now, in memory, seems so huge: how could a family, even large, like hers, eat so much okra? Okra must be picked every day! Not only the okra patch but also the road that ran alongside it that met the larger road up the hill, where the mailbox stood. Not only the mailbox but also the fields on either side of it where so much cotton grew! Not only grew but was subjected to countless hoe assaults and the poisoning of its leaves. A job for small children, this poisoning of cotton plants to kill insects. Mommy was, briefly, one of those small children. Now she wonders: Did the liquid arsenic that splashed on her legs seep into her skin and into her cells? Would it damage her body all these decades later? Had it already done so?

But more important is the return in memory

of your nesting boxes nailed against the smokehouse wall with a stick ladder leading up to them; for here is where Mommy received her first gift from you: your eggs. Eggs to eat with a breakfast of bacon and grits, and then, later, to be used to pay for piano lessons. Because Mommy, from birth, was enchanted by music. There is at last a hazy view of well-perfumed Miss Yarborough, Mommy's teacher, especially of her wispy green dress and freckled tan skin, who charged the fifty cents per lesson Mommy received from the store in town for selling your eggs: a dozen at a time in a paper bag. The eggs were Mommy's mother's gift to her, to her music. But alas, this gift could not last beyond half a dozen lessons; eggs were needed more for food than for music. And so, memory of gathering your eggs, using the ladder to climb and fetch them, balancing on it as it swayed and shook, disappeared from Mommy's mind. As did the journey into town carefully holding the eggs, wedged between her parents' bodies in the front seat of the old blue and white car, as did the face of the man who bought them.

A fence made of hog wire was attached to the side of the smokehouse. Behind it lived hogs and their families. Mommy's parents considered it natural, and of course it was traditional to have male and female hogs who (Mommy prefers "who" to "that") reproduced.

Their pen was large, with trees in the back of it for the privacy hogs required. Hogs who seemed content, for the most part, and who enjoyed a sexual life, which, to the small curious person that Mommy was, seemed astonishing. Though Mommy's parents tried to give them privacy for their very long, passionate, elaborately vocalized entanglements, the hogs did not care for it; they preferred the open space of the pen, nearer to the food trough. Or so it seemed to Mommy. It was amazing to Mommy that the penis of the male hog, though pink, was shaped exactly like a cork screw; and years later, forty or so, she thought: *Oh, is* that *why it is called screwing?* She had wondered.

Their names were casual, given usually because of a physical or spiritual characteristic, as nicknames were given to people: Mr. Greed, Nosy Nell, High Hip, Mistress Sloth, Sir Charleston. The latter a stately pig who seemed to dance on occasion. But, being intelligent, they learned their names quickly, and responded to them. They liked to eat and sleep, make love— meaning have sex—and they liked to snuggle with their young and each other. They enjoyed lying in the mud in the sun and scratching their sides on the fence posts. Their eyes, to Mommy as a child, seemed human, and were sometimes hazel, gray, or pale blue.

All the male pigs suffered when they were

neutered, a ritual Mommy as a small child was not permitted to see. She only heard the anguished squeals, and watched closely, later, as the pigs healed from their ordeal and were given more and tastier food to eat before they were slaughtered: a yearly routine for which her parents prepared with palpable dread. They were losing creatures they liked, creatures they'd talked to and at every day. They would be saying good-bye to personalities they knew, personalities who knew them. Personalities they had known and commented about from birth. Their world would be impoverished by absence of this relationship. And yet, they must eat. Smaller pigs, the offspring of the slain, would replace their parents, very soon.

And then there was Buddy, the bull who kept the same name bull after bull, year after year. Tethered where the grass was best. Stroked and sometimes sung to, led about to find fresh pasture, as if he were a dog. For at least one year. Then there was the day, sadly, when the .22 was brought from behind the wardrobe, and Buddy was petted and stroked and talked to as if he were a person. Thanked for his offering to the family. Then shot while he was still dreaming and munching on fresh grass. His knees would buckle and he would look interrupted. Mommy's brothers would talk about this later. Mommy would have run away by then.

Only to return when Buddy, always a brown or black bull, shiny and plump, was already "meat."

As "meat" he was quite different. Still handled with respect but with more lightness. Neighbors who helped with the butchering laughed as they told stories and shared memories of other events. Every grown-up was busy skinning and cutting "meat." Blood covered their hands but they did not seem to notice. Mommy's parents sent portions of meat to elders and widows with children, grandparents and the ill and shut in. The rest of the carcass (no longer referred to as Buddy) was prepared for the freezer locker in town where it would be kept until it was all gone; hopefully, it would last through the winter. There would be many remembrances of Buddy over countless meals; he would be praised for his good nature in life and his good taste in death.

Mommy could never eat cow or bull when she was a girl. And she always thought of them as gendered beings. For her, the cow was too beautiful to eat. Her breath was sweet, her eyes large, clear, and kind. Her body likewise smelled sweet and was of gentle movement. She gave milk to humans and was passionately attached to her calves. Mommy's parents and brothers, who managed the dairy for the man who owned it, told stories of how desperately the cows fought to keep their calves, how they tried to hide them after they were born. But where could they hide them? Only in the brush and forest so well known to humans.

And then, after college, while living in New York City, Mommy ate "steak." So strange at first it was, but cheap and filling and "good protein" from a place called Tad's Steakhouse. This is where students and others on a restricted budget went to eat: a "steak" and baked potato with salad cost only $1.49. It seemed she was always in the company of people who relished eating "steak"; from their enthusiasm it seemed to be manna from heaven. For many years, at least seven, Mommy ate it sometimes too. She learned to sear it over coals or in a pan, and share it with her friends and family. Sometimes she could honestly say it tasted delicious. She forgot Buddy, completely.

But in order to forget Buddy she had to forget the pine tree under which he was tethered much of the time, the same tree under which he was shot. She had to forget the garden fence where his hide was hung and the okra patch whose edge sprouted fresh grass Buddy had strained, against his rope, to reach. She had to forget how his smoothly ringed horns and silken forehead felt, warmed from the sun; the lively smell of him; and how patient and humble his eyes were, though sometimes thoughtful and even calculating. He seemed to her to have a quiet and pensive inner life. Who was Buddy? How would Buddy have designed his life? As a child she had asked this question endlessly. As a grown-up she had forgotten it.

22

FROM: POEMS FOR MY GIRLS

HOW CAN HUMANITY
look the deer
in
the face?
How can I,
having erected
my fence?

23

GRANDFATHER GANDHI— AND MOMMY'S EXPERIMENTS WITH REALITY

DEAR GIRLS,

Today it is a toss up: whether to write to you about the high quality (and tastiness) of your eggs, which Mommy can't believe she hasn't done before; forgive me! Or, to write to you about my experiments with "meat." I think because I tossed and turned so much last night attempting to digest four bites of lamb, I should write to you about the latter. Grandfather Gandhi in his book *The Story of My Experiments with Truth* says that the last time he ate meat, lamb in fact,

113

he could hear the bleating of the lamb in his stomach for hours. That finished the meat experience for him, permanently. I have a feeling I'm a bit different from Grandfather. (What the heck is a grandfather, you're no doubt wondering, and why is Mommy bringing it up? Is it some kind of collard? Is it a mash? Is it a grain?) No, my darlings, it isn't anything like that: a grandfather, or grandmother, is someone who wants only your health and happiness and he or she doesn't mind in the least being seen as a fool to see that these objectives are achieved. That's Mommy's best definition of these folks. Grandfather Gandhi, for instance, eventually wore only a single piece of homemade cloth wrapped ingeniously around his slight brown frame, went bald, and lost most of his teeth. But did that stop him from traveling to England and presenting himself and the demands of his colonized country to the Queen? No. Well, I don't know if he actually saw the Queen. She's not exactly a grandmother of the kind we're discussing. Too much bloody mash, which rhymes with cash, of which Grandfather Gandhi had barely a cent. But what is cash, you will wonder? Cash is something like mash except you can't eat it. Which means it's completely uninteresting to you! Humans love it though, so much so that they often get a lot of blood in it from all the things they think they have to kill.

Anyway, leaving the pilgrimage of visiting living grandmothers and grandfathers in January, Mommy interrupted her primarily vegetarian diet to have a meal of roast goose that was served by a smiling flight attendant on the plane. It was Lufthansa, this plane (Mommy loves Lufthansa), and its emblem is a goose or maybe a swan in flight! Oh, dear. The goose was delicious and helped Mommy's body and spirit as she crossed the ocean coughing along with several other sufferers on the plane. In fact, it was interesting: every sufferer's cough was exactly the same, a kind of hacking. And everybody, like Mommy, seemed to be either swooning backwards in his or her seat or else going to the bathroom. Intense. So in this case, with the roasted goose, Mommy was fine. She thanked it with all her heart for giving its strength to her when she so needed it. Mommy had learned to avoid most vegetarian meals on planes because in the early days, at least, they seemed to be comprised of two tiny bales of hay with unsweetened applesauce smeared over them. She ordered regular fare and carefully picked her way around the flesh.

The next encounter happened when L., Mommy's daughterly acting neighbor, made two big red pots of chicken soup. Though I could not bring myself to eat the chicken, I very much enjoyed the broth! Again, I thanked L. and I thanked the chickens who had added their strength to mine. Mommy's partner also brought beef stew from the S$\overline{oo}$P shop in Berkeley. The food in this place has a reputation for being from farms where compassion for animals is the rule. Mommy felt energized eating it, rather than depressed.

Then, next encounter a few weeks later: in a restaurant on the beach, I ate a fish, a red snapper, called in Mexico a Huachinango. Again my body seemed to call for a protein heavier than my diet of mostly vegetables and quinoa, fruit and vegetable smoothies, with the occasional support of shrimp and octopus and bits of dorado made into a nice soup. This fish was about the size of my hand and came with its head attached. I felt compassion for its small size, its motherless swimming; who and where was its mother, I wondered? I ate it in a mood of solidarity with all of us taken from our habitats to become "food" of one sort or another to those stronger than we are. Years ago, when I was vegan for five months, I thought I would never be able to eat anything with eyes, but I ate this young fish, every possible bite, with gratitude.

A month later, after a fast and liver cleanse (Mommy loves her liver!) and after meals comprised of many veggies and fruits, I was again presented with a menu. This time, much to the surprise of everyone

at the largely vegetarian table, Mommy ordered curried goat! Again, it seemed to Mommy that her body
saw on the menu what it needed. *Eyes are body too!*
It needed curried goat. This was delicious and very
strengthening, and Mommy was again grateful. She
took some home to eat the next day. She envisioned
the goat, prayed its life was good and its death as painless as possible, and that whoever had lived with it had
understood the miracle that it was. From childhood
Mommy has appreciated the unusual inward staring eyes, resourceful foraging, and musky goat smell
unique to this expression of life.

Mommy was probably the last person on earth to
see the movie *Cold Mountain*, but she finally saw it and
valued it for three reasons: it cured her of her inability to feel compassion for the soldiers who fought on
the Confederate side in the Civil War because it made
one young soldier come vulnerably alive; it showed
how important it was in those days for a family during
winter to have a hog to kill and eat (they were like her
own family); and it showed a wise woman living in the
woods with her goats and how she killed one of them
while its head was in her lap and she was stroking and
lovingly murmuring to it. She then cooked some of the
meat for the wounded soldier to eat. That depiction, of
how killing an animal might be done, is one Mommy

appreciates because it reminds humans that though we must eat other living beings to live, we do not have to withdraw our affection when it is most needed and abandon our sustainers in their moment of transition.

Eating the lamb was different than eating the goose, the chicken, the cow, the fish, or the goat. It was more thoughtless, more whimsical. First Mommy said no, then she said yes, simply because in the mellow light of the restaurant the lamb looked appetizing as it was going around the table. She was hungry and didn't really like the eggplant, veggie samosas, or daal on her plate. After four bites, she realized her mistake. In the middle of the night it did not really surprise her that the lamb—whose entire flock came to look Mommy over as she tossed and turned during the night—would not move farther than her esophagus.

24

A FEW KIND WORDS ABOUT STUPIDITY

DEAREST GIRLS,

Today, coming down the hill to see you after three days of rain, I saw a good-sized buck not far from your house. He was handsome, soft tan and gray, with smart seven- or eight-inch-long antlers. He stood still long enough for me to get a good look and to definitely know that he was there. I could almost see the shine of his dark brown eyes. In the days before you came, long before in fact, there used to be deer families. I could see them from the window of my studio.

This was before I had running water or electricity, and I sometimes saw them when I went outside to water my small flower garden by hand—my neighbors having run a hose and pipeline from their house. We would all stand very still, very quiet, and gaze across the distance at each other. Enchanted. Delighted. Awed. *On my part.* What the deer felt I can't imagine, though they tolerated my presence well enough and continued munching their way across the meadow.

Years later I had both water and electricity and I decided I needed a fence as well; grass and shrubs were not all the deer liked to munch. They liked the succulence of all my flowers, especially the roses; they liked the small apple trees; they liked corn and squash. There was nothing they didn't like. Maybe oleander, with its white and pink and red blooms, beautiful but poisonous. I am glad you have none of this plant within reach because you would certainly peck at it. At least once. Leaving Mommy distraught.

So Mommy constructed her fence. And she did consider the deer. Of forty acres (Mommy bought forty acres and a rototiller instead of forty acres and a mule for reasons that would not interest you at this point) I fenced in ten. This would protect the yard, the orchard, and the garden, I thought. The deer would have a couple of meadows, a forest, and a pond to enjoy. We would coexist. However, Mommy had not factored in the coming of the vineyards that fenced in everything but the narrowest sliver of grass track along the roads, and the coming, as well, of hunters. It was a shock to her to see, over a period of ten or fifteen years, a decimation of the deer population, and to see the sad spectacle of does and their fawns frantically trying to find camouflage and shelter along narrow vineyard-lined roads that offered neither. Attempting to jump out of the way of speeding cars, startled deer frequently crashed into the fence, breaking their necks.

The bucks were routinely hunted by . . . but Mommy can't claim to know who these hunters were. They were people who shot the male deer, the bucks (young black men were called bucks and hunted when they ran away from enslavement in the Old South; Indian men were likewise called bucks and hunted for many years), and placed them over the tops of their cars as they drove back to the city—never noticing apparently how beautiful (left alive) was the being whose life they destroyed—often while drinking beer, smoking cigarettes, and eating candy bars. Beer cans, cigarette butts, and candy wrappers were some of the debris left behind.

There was a family that lived near Mommy who hunted also, but they were often without work and deer meat was a major source of their sustenance, especially during winter. These were indigenous people who chose not to live on a reservation; the discrimination against them, outside the reservation, was strong. Discrimination often means having a hard time finding a place to live or feeding yourself and your family. People could starve. Like, for instance, some of you could starve if I gave food only to the Red Gang of Six (now five, actually) and very little or none to Rhode Island Reds, Barred Rocks, or Ameraucanas.

For a long time Mommy didn't know what to do. This was her stupidity. Often that is what stupidity really is. Not knowing what to do. You see the problem; it troubles your heart; but you have no idea what your part is in making a change. So Mommy was stuck for a couple of years. Seeing fewer and fewer deer, and no intact deer families at all, only terrorized does and bewildered, frightened fawns. Until one night there was a big storm that knocked down part of her beautiful fence. Next morning she saw how eagerly and gracefully deer began to leap through the broken part. *Aha!* She thought. *That's it. The deer and I need a broken fence.* She decided not to repair it. And then to kick down and cut through other sections of the fence as well.

However, some of the old problems returned.

Chewed up roses, munched-to-the-ground apple trees, devoured veggies and fruits. All the things close to her food-growing heart. Even blackberries! And then she realized what she needed to do. The solution came to her in a flash of inspiration, which is simultaneously a welcome release from stupidity! Instead of fencing the deer out, she needed to fence herself in, her and her various gardens and munchables. She saw how she and her kind, humans, were really the dangerous ones. So that is what she did. She drew a snug though graceful circle around her house and yard and fenced that in. She drew another tight and attractive circle around her vegetable garden and fenced that in. Small orchard trees she gave their individual small fences. Altogether this accounted for less than an acre of the land. The deer would have the rest, all thirty-nine acres. Well, she and the deer.

And Mommy waited for deer families to be reunited and return. She especially waited to see a good-sized buck. And today, *hallelujah*, that is what she saw.

By the time I got to your place I was feeling wonderful. For that is what seeing animals in the wild does to us, makes us feel we are alive in Life and living in a paradise filled with moment by moment wonder. And then I saw you. And guess what had happened to some of you in my absence earlier—not of days but of a few weeks? You had grown beards!

25

BEARDED LADIES

COMING UPON YOU after weeks of not seeing you every day, I felt like Penelope taking her first glance at Ulysses. You are all so much bigger, more self-confident and self-assured than when I left, that for a moment Mommy wondered if you were the same chickens. And you appear even more intelligent. Mommy has always thought chickens have a look of erudition; but by now you have a look that is practically professorial. Fleeting, I admit, because usually you are on your way to devouring something: greens, grains, or bugs. But it is there, that look of high intelligence, and Mommy appreciates it. She amused herself imagining you in reading spectacles.

What she did not expect was that the Ameraucanas among you, you of the pale green and blue eggs, would also sprout beards. Beards in the Abe Lincoln style; beards that go up to and seemingly into your ears. What magic is this? Bearded ladies who also lay colorful eggs! The wonder of this leaves Mommy breathless.

The other change is that you are molting. Which means you are throwing off all of your old feathers and new ones are coming through. You are not tidy, not neatly into your ordinarily compact and perfect chicken shape. You look a bit mussed. But you don't seem to notice, which is a lovely trait. Did humans ever have this? Did we ever go through our life changes without making a big deal about them? Did we ever, anywhere, have our hair fall out, new hair grow in, and not once try to find a mirror?

I like your lack of vanity. It is refreshing.

Sometimes, sitting on my green stool and lulled by your complete indifference to the consequences of your natural behaviors, I wish we were more like you. More relaxed with our breasts and bellies and our feathers (of whatever sort) and our heights and weights and how we toss our heads back to drink water or how we sometimes let a leaf of lettuce slip from our fork.

You seem so clear about who you are. So certain that you are just right as you are, that for all your intelligence and maybe in spite of it, you never seem to need a second opinion.

26

IN THE NIGHT MOMMY
HEARS MANGOES FALLING

IN THE NIGHT Mommy hears mangoes falling. They are not bombs. In the morning she collects them in her hat and is led back into the kitchen by a butterfly. To Mommy all of Earth is heaven; this two-minute-long experience is its apex: one of endless many. Of course Mommy thinks of you and how you would like to peck a hole in the plumpest red mango and how you would stand over it gobbling and happy. She would like to bring her whole hatful of mangoes home to you; and maybe she can manage to bring one or two. But no, customs would nab her. A nabbed Mommy is a pitiful thing, as we see in places in the world where Mommies are nabbed regularly and thrown into prisons or servitude when all they are trying to do is get something of value, usually food, to bring home to their children.

Mommy will have to eat a mango for the collective. Which includes you.

Mommy was lying in bed this morning thinking thankfully that no one has been lost from the chicken yard since the sad death of one of the Red Gang of Six. She had been wondering about naming them and had thought, if one were a rooster, she would name him Uncle Ho. Then she would name two others, hens or roosters, Chi and Min. Mommy had a fondness for Uncle Ho, who so completely loved his people and his land. She thought he was as brave as morning: imagine getting up every day to fight invaders all those decades when he would have been happier doing something else. He was a cute little old man, too, and Mommy thinks he must have had chickens. Or thought about chickens, even when the bombs and napalm were falling on his country, Vietnam. He was a poet and they are like that. She thought she'd name the other three Alice B., Toke, and Lass. She thought this would make Gertrude Stein happy. Thinking of those two, Mommy realized (late in the day!) that the expression "toking" or "having a toke," which was popular during the marijuana years of the sixties and seventies, was derived from Alice B. Toklas's name because Alice used to make marijuana brownies and no doubt also took a puff or two while she and Gertrude were enjoying cows. (This is a play on a Stein/Toklas reference to orgasm no doubt lost completely on chickens.)

Mommy was never much of a smoker of anything, though of course she on occasion smoked marijuana; everyone she knew at the time did so. What she liked was the intense connection she felt to the plant itself and in fact to the plant world in general. She was amazed and realized this had to be marijuana's major function; it is a plant that teaches plant love. With this in mind, Mommy immediately planted six plants: three female and three male. The male plants were beautiful but not potent; she felt no special connection to anything while smoking them, which was fascinating to the explorer in Mommy. The female plants were powerful, even when very little, and much more so when they grew tall, well over Mommy's head. They were so powerful in their scent, a scent that was so familiar, that Mommy immediately called them Grown Women. It was years before she understood that Mexicans had long ago noticed this scent, and that this is the reason they called the plant Mary Jane. If she had gotten it earlier, while she was toking, she would have laughed and laughed, which is something else marijuana made her do. And of course it made her munch like a fiend.

27

HI, GLADYS, GLADYS, GLADYS, GLADYS, GLADYS

IT TURNS OUT, Mommy realized, after many days watching them, that she still could not tell any of the Gang of Five apart. Unlike the Barred Rocks with their crisp black-and-white swirls of feathers, or the Ameraucanas with their vivid colors and distinctive designs, the Rhode Island Reds, which is what the gang consisted of, all looked pretty much alike. Of course to them this would not be the case! Among the gang, as among Africans, Asians, Europeans, etc., each individual would look completely different. Humans like to think all humans of another race look alike, but that is because the glance of the uncaring stranger tends to be superficial. Mommy was neither a stranger nor uncaring; she still had a hard time telling the girls apart. What she did notice, however, is that seeing them in all their russet glory always made her feel glad. Glad to see them, glad to witness their merger into the frequently ruthless pecking order of the chicken yard, glad to find them beginning to cackle and to lay eggs.

What else would their name be but Gladys?

And that is what she named all of them.

A bonus of naming them Gladys was the sound of her call to them: *Hi, Gladys, Gladys, Gladys, Gladys, Gladys.* It reminded Mommy a bit of the turkey's call to its mate, though less of a gobble, of course. It also sounded like something the chickens themselves would make up. Spoken rapidly it became a song. The chickens liked it: Mommy could tell. They ran up to meet her at the gate to their yard when she called to them, responding with a chorus or two—not quite in the same key—of their own.

28

AUTOMATIC

DEAR GIRLS,

Last night I killed a spider, not just any spider but a Mommy spider with all of her little ones underneath her body. How did this happen? Mommy saw what she thought was a dead cockroach in the corner of the shower. Taking a tissue, she scooped it up, noticing as she did so that there were a lot of tiny creatures apparently feeding on the body. By the time she'd put the "dead cockroach" in the toilet, along with some of the little creatures, the spider had gained enough strength to wiggle a leg, and on closer inspection Mommy could see that the tiny things she thought were eating the dead body of the cockroach were indeed baby spiders. In one motion she had dropped the spider in the toilet and hit the flush button, before noticing what she was doing.

Now you of course would have snapped up the spider in a bite, no qualms at all. But Mommy isn't a chicken this lifetime and she has a few. Why didn't she pay more attention? What was her hurry? She thought of Daddee, who is her teacher very often in situations of this sort. He would never have killed the spider, especially not by drowning, which must be a terrible way to die. Instead he would have taken the big spider outside, along with as many little spiders as he could, and placed them on the grass. This would have taken a few seconds. Mommy is mindful in this way too, most of the time, but at other times she shifts into automatic. In "automatic," bugs of any kind are suspect: cockroaches are germ-ridden; fleas are beneath thought; and spiders have been known to bite and leave black-and-blue marks, not to mention soreness and swelling.

For Mommy, spiders, ticks, mosquitoes, and scorpions are the hardest life forms with which to resonate. Chickens eat all of them, which is incredible to contemplate. Mommy wonders: Don't they bite, sting, attach, and suck on something inside? Or are your digestive juices powerfully acidic and all critters liquefied before they have a chance to do harm? Daddee says your gizzards contain gravel that does the crushing and grinding work: but isn't your gizzard a fair distance from your throat? Mommy imagines a scorpion stinging like crazy all the way down.

Mommy's mind is dizzy and her heart sore from all the troubles in the human realm. She sees pictures of other birds, no less wondrous than you, covered with oil and dying of suffocation and despair. How can they fathom what is happening to them? How can they understand they are not to blame? What have they done but be themselves, flying about eating insects and grubs, while appearing marvelous to the human spirit, even while doing so? She learns soldiers from her country have shot and killed two pregnant women in Afghanistan, one of them Mommy of ten. What is an Afghanistan? You will wonder. Is it edible? Mommy has never been there, but she used to wear beautiful long dresses made of velvet and embroidered in many colors, which came from Afghanistan. She did not know these magical dresses were so inexpensive because the country of Afghanistan even then, forty years ago, was being destroyed so that humans could grab the same kind of oil now drenching and drowning innocent beings that remind her of you. What would you like there: other chickens, maybe, though you'd fight to establish and maintain a pecking order; but maybe you'd like the melons and the tomatoes. Maybe you'd look up once in a while to see the kites the children fly. Maybe you would think the kites were birds that had somehow managed to be free. Maybe you would not notice the strings.

Mommy's mind goes to trampled nests, plowed-under burrows, once-sheltering shrubs and trees knocked down, trashed, and burned. The very real homes of very real beings hidden or made distant she thinks by the word "habitat." Some people think it is enough that humans don't eat meat, but this avoids consideration of all the animals murdered in their beds as land is cleared to grow veggies and grain. Grain and veggies, and fruit too, that you, my girls, and vegetarian humans enjoy. The animals that are killed or run off their land so that grapes can be made into the wine most people love to drink would have a lot to say, if they could speak, about our murder of them. Mommy is thankful we don't make wine from the grapes of our three vines; we eat them. But what about the land and creatures smothered by oil and killed because humans have cars and trucks to run? And wars to fight to maintain a global pecking order that has those at the top sitting on most of the mash?

Sometimes Mommy wonders: Is the human species a test? As much as she adores it, she can see it has no idea, generally speaking, where it is, or how to live here.

If Mommy could bring the Mommy spider back to life she would pick her up gently, if at arm's length, and place her outside on the grass, her and her babies. But that particular spider is gone, leaving SPIDER still here. Just as when a human dies, he or she is gone but HUMANITY remains. Which means whatever is learned can be considered, absorbed, and in the future (or the present) put to use on whatever or whoever is left behind.

That is the prayer.

29

ATTACHMENT

GIRLS!

Horrific news! I read today that Mommy should not be eating eggs; that they are acidic and bad for Mommy's health. How can this be? I am not sure I can ever stop eating eggs, especially eggs that came through you.

Mommy is reminded of flying in planes with Daddee and carrying your eggs with us. What is a "planes" you may well ask. Well, a plane is something almost exactly like a very, very large chicken. It flies, just as you do, only much higher in the sky and faster. Even faster than a hawk it flies. And it makes a lot of noise, too, but it flies so far from grass and straw and bugs and other things with which you are familiar that it can't be heard. I know this sounds crazy.

Anyhoo, the point is that Daddee and Mommy never leave home without a nice stash of your eggs. Mommy boils them the night before a trip, and packs as well a bit of sea salt. What is sea? What is salt? Sea is where everything was born! Isn't that the coolest? And it's a really big container of water; you would hardly grasp its size since the water you know intimately comes from a hose attachment that leads into your watering tray. Salt? Something that makes other things taste better but isn't all that good for you. I'll bring you some salted peanuts to try. But in the same book I learn I should give up peanuts too. Even peanut butter! Acid, again. But Mommy loves peanuts and peanut butter, though I have noticed feeling a bit uncomfortable after eating them. Maybe I should stop reading this book before I find out why pecans and I must part company.

So, anyway, there Daddee and Mommy sit, inside this giant chicken; and we are waiting to see if anything on our food tray is going to be edible. Daddee soldiers on, usually, with whatever is put before him; but Mommy almost always has to rely on the comfort of our egg stash. Sometimes Daddee joins Mommy and we have a picnic at which you are sweetly present.

Sometimes, peeling an egg at thirty thousand feet. Don't ask. It's high. Peeling an egg way up in the sky (which humans used to think was a place called heaven) I will say: *Oh, I think this must be Hortensia's egg. The shell is so tough!* Or, Daddee will say: *Whose egg do you think this is?* If the shell is green or blue I know it is from Splendor II, Babe II, or maybe Gertrude Stein. If it is large and brown, it could be from Gladys or Gladys or Gladys, etc. Or even from Rufus.

We sit munching your eggs and I just love you more with every bite. What a gift you have given us! Saving us from who-knows-what rubbery flesh and un-palatable greens. But there was a moment when I had to laugh at the humanness of myself: the old attach-ment question. After eating our eggs we were of course left with a small pile of shell fragments. The flight at-tendant was coming along asking for any trash. We gave him our napkins and our plastic cups, our orange peels (Mommy brought oranges and apples too), and our crumpled *New York Times* (which Mommy reads sometimes when she travels), but I could not for the life of me hand over your eggshells. When the flight attendant reached for them, neatly enclosed in a paper napkin, I found myself placing a hand over them.

Daddee smiled.

I cannot bear to have them go just anywhere, I said.

I understand, said Daddee.

We will take them with us, I declared, *everywhere we go on this trip (which might be a month long), and I will bring them home again and either put them in the compost or make calcium tea for the houseplants out of them.*

Excellent idea, said Daddee.

And so, Mommy ate your eggs, carrying a bit of you inside her for part of a day, and when she came home she carefully tucked your eggshells deep into the compost. Compost is where Mommy herself will be someday; maybe our calcium will completely merge.

30

MOMMY WRITES ABOUT HORTENSIA

DEAR FEATHERED MYSTERIES,

Girls!

Yesterday when Mommy came to collect eggs and to throw you fresh greens over the garden fence, she noticed Hortensia running into the chicken house to sit on a nest. She did not budge while Mommy collected eggs. When Mommy came close to her nest, and was reaching for an egg in a nest close by, all the chickens from the yard crowded round to watch her; they seemed upset. She could tell by the quarreling, even aggressive, sounds they made; looking at her all the while with baleful eyes. Before she could lay her hand on the egg she was about to put in her egg basket, Hortensia wheeled around in her nest, surrounded now by five or six other chickens, including Babe II, Splendor II, Glorious II, Rufus, Agnes of God, and Gertrude Stein, and pecked a hole in the egg she had been sitting on and proceeded to slurp it up. Mommy had no idea a chicken could slurp. But as she watched, all of you tackled whatever parts of the dripping egg yolk and white you could reach and you ate it to the shell. Mommy was stunned.

It's true Daddee had told her about finding empty eggshells in the nests before: he thought blue birds were the culprit. Maybe blue jays, who are known to be predatory and territorial. They will eat the eggs of other birds, in order to leave more space and food for their own offspring. Daddee thought the birds had flown in through the wire that covers the top of the yard, and had gone into the chicken house and pecked holes in whatever eggs they found. That you, coming back to your nests, had found these opened-up and delicious eggs, and had learned how to open them yourselves and to eat them.

I recalled how you looked at me when I first began collecting your eggs, months ago when they were still small, a bit larger than a golf ball. Now they are as big as any in the supermarket, which amazes Mommy. You had a puzzled look: What's she doing? You seemed to ask. What's the deal with collecting those roundish weird things that drop out of us any time we sit for a spell? By the way, Mommy learned something during this period that just astounded her: that your eggs don't come out of you hard; they transition to hardness as they are being expelled. Mommy thinks the Earth and humans should stop spinning long enough to consider this; it certainly made her wonder more than ever how humans ever wandered into this magical realm.

But I digress.

Hortensia, Mommy realized, was what humans used to call a ringleader. A rebel. A cynic and revolutionary. And Mommy thought about the ways Hortensia exhibited her comprehension of her captive situation, and that of her sister chickens, and how she had steadfastly expressed her disdain. It was Hortensia who never warmed to Mommy. Hortensia who took cracked corn from Mommy's hand, yes, but always managed to bite her finger or peck at her well-oiled and therefore shiny shins. (She shared this trait with Rufus.) It was Hortensia who refused to make nice with visitors to the yard, choosing to hang back in a corner while humans oohed and aahed and exhibited usually not one bit of intelligence about chicken behavior.

Mommy had thought Hortensia merely antisocial. But now she thought of her more insightfully as perhaps an existentialist. Life was absurd, of course, here in the chicken yard and hen house, which denied access to a larger world seemingly packed with predators, but there were still choices to be made. Not for her the pretense of contentment with her lot, but not for her also the lack of awareness exhibited by some of the chickens, that there was simply nothing she could do. She *could* do something, even as a captive chicken whose product, eggs, was being mercilessly exploited by a human who thought of herself as kindhearted. She could peck the hand that fed her; she could bite the exposed shin that wandered near her well-sharpened beak. She could sit on her eggs as long as she could and damn it, if it came to that, she could jolly well eat them herself.

This would have been the first chicken to go into the pot, when Mommy was a girl and sent out into the yard to chase down a chicken and wring its neck. This would have happened when Mommy was nine or ten. In Mommy's right hand, from that time so long ago, there still lives the imprint of a chicken's severed head. She could almost remember the rest of it: the wringing motion of her own small arm and hand, the release of the body of the chicken as it separated from its head, the sickening moment of watching the body of the chicken jump about as if unaware it had no head. What had watching this done to Mommy? Where are children required to place such images? *Quit running around like a chicken with its head cut off.* That's partly where it went, that scene, that experience. Into a folk expression. It became simply a fact of life. Humans laughed about it. And yet, the head of the chicken, the imprint of the head, remained in Mommy's hand. It lives there to this day.

Mommy could hardly look at Hortensia, or at any of you, when she realized your awareness. What could she do?

She sat on her meditation camping chair that is fading from the sun and watched your life. *If I were a chicken what would I want right now?* She asked herself. *I would want to be let out of here, for sure*, was the answer. So Mommy called Miles the dog to help her and she let all of you out into the garden. With her deer-headed stick and Miles's herding instinct and swashbuckling bushy tail, a bit of order was maintained as you tore into the wider enclosed space, searching for worms and bugs and the occasional onion start and randomly sampled or shat-upon strawberry.

31

MOMMY IS SO THANKFUL
TO HAVE YOU APPEAR

THE TRUTH IS that millions of small humans are injured and maimed every year. Where do they go when they are hurt? What happens to them that nobody sees? I am so thankful to have you appear in my life to remind me of where I went, what happened to me, when I was only a little human, and suffering. It felt to Mommy as though she suddenly fell down a deep hole. Deeper than the holes you dig for your daily dust baths. That life continued to swirl above and around her, but she was no longer part of it. And that is why you became so important to her, though she would not begin to know this until years later, one night as she was wandering home from a fire dance in a village in Bali. She saw you and was strong enough (finally!) to revisit the deep hole into which she had fallen, and lived, for many years. There was something about you that struck her. It was your beauty, of course, your grace and capable behavior as mother hen to many small chicks, but more terrifyingly perhaps, Mommy was on her way to recalling a chicken's severed head, the impression of which lived in her palm. But what was the connection?

Mommy believes it is this: that when small children are injured they do in fact leave their bodies. She thinks of children she sees around the world who have lost arms and legs and eyes and hands and parts of their faces (trauma deliberately inflicted by others); she knows from experience that they are no longer really there, though their bodies remain. This is why many old humans have said: Never abuse or harm a child, because s/he may go away so far s/he may never come back. Sometimes, too, Mommy thinks, in that "far elsewhere" place the child's spirit roams, it becomes unstuck from humanity, and terrible things are done, almost as if the human, who is now adult, is fast asleep. What happened to Idi Amin, Mommy wonders? Saddam Hussein? Hitler and his imitators? The torturers of Abu Ghraib? Men who stone women? People who cage animals for years on end, or, in the interest of "science," murder and dissect them? What happened to elected officials who say yes to bombing people who from the air appear to be frightened and scurrying ants? If Mommy could explain to you how humans might be mistaken for ants, she would. As for bombing, it is like throwing the biggest stone imaginable, except when you drop a bomb you don't stone one person but thousands. What is a stone? It is a rock. And you would know it from trying to pull worms or insects, often in pieces, from underneath it.

There was your head in Mommy's palm. And perhaps this happened close to the moment she herself was injured. In any case, now she understands that it was her own head that she lost the day she was injured. That it was she herself left to "run around like a chicken with its head cut off." And that she lived that way for many years, headless, though no one around her at the time seemed to notice.

Mommy completely lost those years with her family, because she was not there. And, not being there, she could not appreciate how they suffered, too, along with her. She could not see, or pay attention to, the fact that they loved her.

If they had not loved her they would not have moved back to a more familiar community than the community in which she was injured, which had afforded them a somewhat nicer dwelling than the one closer to Mommy's schoolmates and cousins and grandparents; the shack Mommy hated. If they had not loved her they would not have worked endless hours to pay for pretty dresses and sturdy shoes they made sure she always wore. They would not have filled large platters with fried chicken and placed them first in front of her; any sibling who reached for Mommy's favorite piece of chicken, the drumstick, was smacked on the hand. But Mommy could see mostly the inside of the hole and then the far elsewhere country in which she floated as spirit. Spirit detached from the child she was to her family.

But with your help, my girls, Mommy is gaining on her fleeing memories. Like one of her beloved inspirations, Virginia Woolf, to whom writing was sometimes like trying to catch a dragonfly, she imagines herself stumbling along behind her memories, hoisting a net.

There is her father, for instance, right at the edge of a huge field that he is plowing. He is a small roast-coffee or fig-colored man with flawless skin and enormous, soulful eyes, and the field is so large he cannot see the end of it. He is behind a mule that is as tired as he is, and he is patiently turning over the soil, furrow by furrow. Mommy sees herself bringing cool well water to him in a Mason jar. He drinks, wipes his brow, smiles at her and explains something about the mule or the field or the clouds or the sun. Then he bends again to his work, which only nightfall will end.

This steadfastness is love.

He might have fled, like so many men, to the North. He might have left his family to fend for themselves. He might have been unable to bear knowing his beloved little daughter had fallen down, alone, into a scary deep hole. A hole that perhaps he knew from his own childhood: his mother had died in his arms of a gunshot wound when he was a boy; this was an injury, a psychological maiming. His father's mother, Sally, had died of unknown causes while *he* was still a child, so, no grandmother; a second psychic distortion— caused by her absence. The necessity, after his mother Kate's death, of caring for five younger siblings; so, little chance for school, for education: a third and formidable injury to someone who should have grown up to study physics and philosophy. To hold forth in universities and coffee houses, rising late and happily rumpled in the mornings to enjoy a latte and croissant with the rest of the dreaming, envisioning world.

Mommy gets it, though clarity has been delayed.

Now she feels in her own heart the love she felt separated from at the time. Her heart embraces, envelops her father; and tears almost fall on the computer in her lap. She is becoming an old woman, older than her father ever was, an amazement in itself: it feels late, but she knows Life teaches as and when it will.

She realizes something else: the love her father and her family gave her is the love she has had to give to others, and to herself. That they successfully overcame her oblivion, her absence and confusion, humbles her.

Mommy wishes she could wake up her dead parents and siblings and tell them her news. But maybe they know already because when she imagines them, they are all smiling indulgently, exactly as they used to smile when she, the youngest, informed them of some other marvelous mystery all of them already knew.

32

GERTRUDE'S NECK

DEAREST GIRLS,

A few weeks ago, when Daddee came north to visit you and to be sure you are OK, while I was far elsewhere, he reported that all was well, except for the curious condition of Gertrude Stein's neck. Some feathers had been lost from her lovely full ruffle, and when he held her close he was able to see that a small part of her neck was exposed. When I arrived home from my wanderings, I saw that this was true. Gertrude Stein had lost a big clump of feathers at the back of her neck, leaving her looking vulnerable and far less stately. Mommy was alarmed.

Her mind immediately found her own Mommy when she was a child: there was her Mommy, Miss Minnie Lou, and she was dressed in the wonderful pink and white outfit she sometimes wore, much to her children's delight, to church. She appeared to them then as a giant Easter egg and delectable wedding cake all in one. It seemed that when she wore this crisp and colorful ensemble the very wilderness in which they sometimes felt they lived should rise up and bow. She would rub her lips with lip rouge (as she called it) and, if she could find it among the odds and ends scattered there, dust her strong and lovely face with a bit of face powder from a small box on the dresser. There would also be a dash of perfume, Evening in Paris, dabbed daintily behind each ear.

To the applause that was the admiration in her children's and their father's eyes, she seated herself carefully in the front seat of the white and blue Packard, ready to go. However, as if to balance the power of her elegance in the most no-nonsense way, and with her white patent leather handbag dangling from her left arm, which also held flowers for various graves she would visit in the cemetery, she carried in her right hand, covered in a glove of sparkling white, the enormously heavy, double-bladed, family ax.

The ax was to cut bark from the red oak tree that grew in the churchyard. After the service, after the eating of barbecue and Brunswick stew, and the drinking of ice-cold lemonade, for which "the men" were mostly responsible, she would deftly lift her skirt above the knee, plant a shiny white slipper firmly on a root of the tree near its base, and proceed to chop away until she had collected a double handful of chips. At home she boiled these chips until they rendered a thick red liquid that she mixed with the drinking water of her chicks: a cure for chicken cannibalism.

So Mommy, your Mommy, was thinking: *Is someone eating, or trying to eat, Gertrude's neck? Is someone pecking her on the neck in an effort to frighten, terrorize, or dominate her? Is she being attacked? Who might the culprit(s) be? And why would there be cannibalism among the chickens anyway, since the greatest cause of cannibalism in chickens is insufficient space.*

Our space is ample. Thought Mommy. A bit proudly.

Mommy tossed and turned, worrying that Gertrude was being abused by the other chickens. She blamed herself for the fact that Gertrude had always been something of a favorite, not just with her and Daddee but with J. and K., Mommy's helpers, who also liked to hold her. Had the other chickens noticed, and had they attacked Gertrude Stein out of jealousy?

Then again, and this truly bothered Mommy, Gertrude Stein had always been the smallest chicken, and if truth be told, the one who seemed to exhibit the most tender feelings. Mommy remembered how devastated Gertrude Stein had been when Bobbie, her best friend, was eaten by the Predator Inhaler. How she appeared to grieve and to long for Bobbie, for weeks. The wistful look on her face, and how, since then, she had seemed lonely and alone. Oh, Mommy could hardly stand it!

In the night, when Daddee was sound asleep, Mommy was dreaming up ways to protect Gertrude Stein. Daddee thought the best way to do that would be to have Gertrude Stein move up the hill to their yard where she would have space and peace to gather herself, and to regrow her neck feathers. He thought Miles the dog could protect her from predators and that at night she could roost in a tree. But Mommy thought that wouldn't work because most predators can climb trees. Miles the dog, part coyote himself, can also climb trees to a certain height but not to the same height as a bobcat or a raccoon or a mountain lion. Or even a porcupine. Besides, Mommy thought that isolating Gertrude Stein, who was being attacked, was not just. The bully is the one to be isolated, she thought. The attacker, not the attacked. She could not bear the thought that Gertrude Stein would be lonely in a new environment that she would have to learn, and that at night she would find sleep difficult because she would have to remain aware of danger.

Mommy thought and thought.

Finally she realized her imagination was running away with her. That what she needed to do was go into the chicken yard, sit down, and stay for an hour or so every day. Just observing the lay of the land. If she watched closely enough, she thought, she would see what was happening to Gertrude Stein and why she had lost those feathers from her neck. And that is what she did.

33

THE FIRST DAY

DEAR GIRLS,

As soon as Mommy sat down to observe what was going on with Gertrude and those missing feathers at the back of her neck, she realized how tired she was. Mommy comes from a long line of people who were forced to work almost every moment they were awake (they were called slaves, though of course they weren't slaves to themselves but rather the enslaved); there was a saying in her parents' household when she was growing up: idle hands are the devil's workshop, though enslavement of people of color had ended a hundred years earlier.

Mommy thought of patterns of behavior, how ingrained they can be, how unnoticed also, though there we are, stuck in them, frequently without knowing. She had always worked hard and actually loved it; it was simply a part of her. *But gosh*, she thought, as she settled into her meditation camping chair, *how tiring working so much of the time could be!* Her ancestors who had no choice about when and where to work were often in her ear advising her to chill, but she was usually too headstrong and stubborn to listen.

She thought of all the hammocks she owned and how she enjoyed them, also of how little time she actually spent suspended in their deliciousness. It was curious, this self-observation, and for some reason, maybe because you were beginning to dig into your dust holes and nestle in the earth for naps, it made her sleepy.

She decided to put her feet up. For this, she needed to take down the green stool and place it under her legs. Settling into this position was heaven. Several of you: Agnes of God, Splendor II, Babe II, and a couple of Gladyses came close and hunkered down beside the chair. There was a fifteen-minute pause in everyone's activities. Mommy knew it wouldn't last and that was fine with her. She wanted to see what was going on between Gertrude Stein and everybody else.

Before she drifted off though she thought about the bliss of sitting with you, how unexpected it was, how exquisite. Did the rest of the world not know about this? Had humans known about it—sitting blissed out with chickens—and somehow lost it? The peace. *The sense of being in sync with the entire enchilada*. Her mind drifted to the ease with which, sitting with chickens, one slipped off the wheel of samsara. There it went, rolling down the hill, and the observer not caring a flying husky one way or another.

Mommy was already delighted by the thought of not coming back around again in human form— what a blessing that was—but she had mused over the possibility of coming back as Something: maybe a hummingbird or butterfly. Maybe a carrot or zucchini. Maybe a breeze. A breeze was probably her favorite. But now she knew Nothing at All would be just fine. Like a long, long sleep in perfect darkness that never ended.

As she was thinking this, she was also looking at Gertrude Stein who was scratching deep into the dust bowl she'd made and fluffing her feathers until they were saturated with dust. It was so lovely to Mommy that chickens had sense enough to know clean dirt wasn't dirty. That you could bathe in it. Next to her was Rufus, who resembled Bobbie, the soul mate she'd lost, and Mommy wondered if their similar markings (both Bobbie and Rufus were Barred Rock) made her more acceptable to Gertrude Stein. Or perhaps Rufus was the one pulling out her feathers.

However, nothing alarming seemed to be happening now.

What happened soon though, maybe because the chicken yard became so quiet, is that a bluish bird with a long beak, not, Mommy thought, a blue jay, alighted on top of the chicken house. It eyed Mommy and the snoozing or dust-bathing chickens. Mommy pretended to be asleep, but she kept her eyes peeled under nearly closed lashes. The bird seemed to understand the scene and, instead of flying down from its perch and into the coop where the eggs were, it flew off. Complaining to its partners, whom Mommy could not see, as it went.

There's a human in there! It seemed to shriek. Bummer!

After napping and bathing, everyone staggered up again and began to question Mommy about whether she had some treats. *You're already very fat*, she said, but in fact, in her backpack, she had brought down a few pieces of corn on the cob. She wondered if you would like it slightly cooked as much as you liked it raw. You did.

Mommy has a horror of blaming anyone for something they haven't done, and so she couldn't be sure the bird was guilty, as she thought might be the case, of pecking holes in the eggs of the chickens. How was she to find out?

34

DAY TWO

ELEMENTARY, MY DEAR girls, elementary!

The first thing Mommy did when she came the second day was consider where she could put a television for you to watch. She'd heard chickens like television. She wondered what it was you liked about it. Maybe the shininess of it and maybe because the shiny things within the shininess moved a lot. She wondered if you'd peck at it. Yes, you would. Mommy herself never learned how to watch television; every time she tried it sucked her in. She wasn't strong enough for it, at all, and was thankful she understood that. She was saving television and remarriage for her very old age. Seen from a distance they both seemed quite nice. Nice, a word Mommy never finds much use for. For some reason it makes her think of pickles.

She still loves Daddee with all her heart, though. So, not to worry.

She thought of Thomas Hardy and how she appreciates his working-class characters and how, in the BBC production of *The Mayor of Casterbridge*, in the very first scene, opening each segment of the story, there is a flock of free chickens running about the yard. She wondered if this might be a program suitable for you. But then she wondered if you'd even recognize the chickens as chickens and kin, though nineteenth-century kin, and whether the rest of the story would have any relevance at all. Well.

She didn't see how she could rig up a television set, though she was happy that you have both electric lights and a wall heater, but maybe she could bring her laptop and treat you to the occasional podcast of *Democracy Now*? You could peck at Juan Gonzalez's glasses and Amy Goodman's shiny silver necklace. Then she thought about *Nurse Jackie*, whose story she had received via Netflix, and how you could help

Nurse Jackie gobble up those pills that keep falling out of the cabinet at the hospital.

Mommy collected all the eggs, first thing. Before sitting. Before sharing treats. Before anything. She collected them in her egg basket that was made in Ghana and has all the subtle seriousness of that artistic, though too-hot-for-Mommy, country. Having collected them, she placed the basket outside the chicken house on top of two bales of straw. Then she settled into her meditation camping chair and put her feet up on the green stool and set herself to observing the scene.

Gertrude Stein, she noted, bobbed about here and there, plucky and matronly and certainly not exhibiting one iota of being a hacked down or diminished soul. She was like a thrifty shopper in the market, choosing each morsel she put into her mouth with dignity and care. When one of the Gladyses attempted to snatch up a grain of Whatever It Was Gertrude Stein had her eye on, Gertrude Stein dive-bombed her, making an almost audible *thunk* against *her* neck. *Somehow*, Mommy mused, *I don't think being attacked by the other chickens is Gertrude Stein's problem.*

Mommy realizes she overuses the word enchantment when she writes about you, but that is the truth of the time she spends sitting with you. The world could end in a thunderclap and she would hardly stir. She loves the way you drift over to her chair and how you nestle close beside her for your naps. You do that funny squat that you also do when she chases you around the garden, just before she picks you up to return you to your yard. But now, instead of simply squatting, with wings stiffly elbowed out, you fluff out your feathers, peck underneath them, and snack on any critter you might be harboring; sometimes you appear to lose your head, holding it for several seconds, serious and intent, under a wing.

But what charms Mommy is how happy you seem to be to feel her presence on the chair beside you. Actually Mommy would sit on the ground but the low-slung chair gives her perfect support should any of you decide to jump on her knees or on her shoulder, which brings you closer to her earrings and glasses. You have an interesting habit too of pecking her clothing on which there is nothing visibly edible. Mommy thinks maybe this is the way chickens show affection, and why a kiss among humans is sometimes called a peck.

Time passes and Mommy knows she is drifting, with you, in Eternity. That this is what being present really means.

When she prepares to leave, after an hour has stretched to an hour and a half, she almost forgets the egg basket she left outside the yard on top of the bales of straw. Taking it down she notices one of the eggs has been pecked open by a bird she did not even see.

Perhaps it was the complaining bird of yesterday who returned unobserved to watch her collect the eggs and place them outside the chicken yard. It saw its chance and took it. At least now she knows who is responsible for breaking into *some* of the eggs, if not for eating them. That bird, or another. She had noticed that one of the chickens napping closest to her chair the past two days, and blinking up at her from time to time with a look of sweet innocence, is Hortensia.

35

LOOKING DEEPLY

GIRLS,

Once upon a time when I was a girl I went to stay with a friend whose husband was a batterer. I knew he had battered my friend while they still lived in Georgia, but now, in New York, my friend assured me he was a new man and never so much as threatened her. She walked about the apartment they shared with an air of freedom and confidence. Mommy was relieved.

And fooled.

It took weeks to realize that the air of freedom

and confidence exhibited by her friend ebbed and flowed, that when she wasn't drifting about the place looking peaceful and content, she was busily attuned to her husband's moods and constantly trying to avoid interaction with him.

So it was with Gertrude Stein. As Mommy was to discover.

Thinking of her friend from so many years ago, Mommy had decided to sit with you twice in one day, once in the morning and once in the afternoon.

In the morning all went well; there was the joy of freshness in the garden, as Mommy tilled and watered, while everyone in the flock pursued her own course. Ever so much scratching and scattering of mulch as the search for insects and seeds kept you busy. No time to fuss or fight. But in the afternoon, enclosed once more in the chicken yard, with Mommy sitting attentive but still and silent on her little chair, it was quite different. For one thing she noticed Gertrude Stein was spending quite a bit of time behind her chair. Was she hiding?

Mommy moved her chair to one side. Gertrude Stein came out into the yard but studiously avoided going near Rufus who was occupied eating the last bit of corn from an ear Mommy had brought for the flock to share. Rufus had cornered it and everybody else stayed away. When she'd finished with it, the rest of the flock approached. But not, Mommy noticed, Gertrude Stein, who, as Rufus moved about the yard, managed to stay at least three feet out of reach.

Her body language was striking. She seemed to shrink into her feathers, to become smaller, like Mommy's friend who could appear to be two different people depending on her husband's moods.

When Mommy drew some sunflower seeds from her pocket and tossed them into the yard, Gertrude Stein had barely made a dash for them before Rufus, head lowered like a battering ram, ran her off. She darted behind Mommy's chair and stayed there.

Mommy was annoyed by this aggression. When she saw Rufus harassing another chicken over a bit of carrot in a corner, she threw a clay egg at her. She had collected the fake eggs out of the nests and was cleaning them with a towel. She missed everything but the ground, of course, but was intrigued to see how interested in the egg everyone became, seeming disappointed that, peck on it as they would, it failed to crack.

What to do? Not about the fake egg, but about Gertrude Stein.

What in fact to do about the bullies of the world? Mommy pondered. This was a serious problem, a humanitarian issue of vital importance, in Mommy's opinion; Rufus was not the only creature on the planet making others hide behind chairs.

I wonder what would happen if we sent the bully away? She mused. Thinking of global human bullies while considering the fate of Rufus.

Someplace secure and kind, for Rufus, she thought, but where she would not have her usual friends and familiar surroundings. Where she would have to learn a few things, like how to be the only chicken among strangers and how to find a safe place to lay her eggs. A place perhaps where there was a dog just territorial enough to keep her on her toes. A place where food was less generously provided, and not easily commandeered by her.

And so, Mommy sent Rufus away to spend a few days with friends and their children and their dog to see if being away from Gertrude Stein, Agnes of God, Splendor II, Babe II, Glorious II, Hortensia, and the Gladyses, and away, as well, from an overindulgent Mommy, might encourage her to diminish or discard her egocentric and aggressive attitude.

36

EVEN BULLIES ARE MISSED AND LOVED

BELOVED SISTER TRAVELERS on the journey,

The first thing Mommy noticed, after Rufus was sent away, was how relaxed everyone else became. Especially Gertrude Stein, who puffed out her feathers until she looked twice her size; but not just Gertrude exuded an air of freedom, everyone else did as well. A calm descended on the chicken yard.

Mommy's human friends reminded her gently that the pecking order among chickens was real: that the domineering behavior she had witnessed, and felt distressed by, had to do with some primordial chicken DNA that she could expect to do nothing about. Chickens insisted on having a honcho at the head of things, they said; a clutch of gang members who followed the leader in the middle; and then, at the end of the line of command, the smallest and apparently weakest of the flock, very often a solitary being, who was fair game for anyone who wanted to attack.

Mommy didn't deny this perceived reality, but because of her own history of being one among those considered at the bottom of the human pecking order, she found it intolerable. Something in her could not bear to let any other creature suffer just because they were smaller and weaker. Besides, bullies were incredibly ugly, she thought, whether human or chicken, and it was an act of liberation for them and an introduction to them of their beauty to assist them in mending their ways.

What Mommy had not expected was the behavior of Agnes of God, sidekick and sister ruffian of Rufus. During the first four days Rufus was gone, she rarely left her nest. She had started out mingling with the other chickens, but halfheartedly. She seemed stunned by their expressions of freedom and lack of fear. She had dive-bombed and pecked every other chicken in the yard, with Rufus right there, backing her up. Now

Rufus had mysteriously vanished. Her flank, therefore, was exposed. She took to her bed.

Mommy came into the coop to gather eggs. *Agnes*, she said, *what's up with you?*

Agnes made no reply, except to sit more stolidly, forlornly, on her nest.

It was clear to Mommy that she was missing Rufus. Mommy wondered how that configured in Agnes of God's mind? How would it feel to her to lose the only being in the world who looked, smelled, and behaved like her?

Mommy felt her heart begin to soften to both Agnes and Rufus. She thought of the good things they did: They protected the flock as well as they could from intruders. They gave every visitor a wicked going over to be sure they were harmless. They were not afraid to jump up in a human's face if the human got too close to the other chickens. They were splendid guardians. *Why*, Mommy wondered, *did being a guardian turn them into tyrants?*

So she e-mailed her friends and asked them to bring Rufus home. Would she have learned a lesson in humility, kindness, and restraint? Mommy could only hope.

37

HA HA, HA HA, HA HA!

DEAREST GIRLS,

Ha Ha, Ha Ha, Ha Ha!

That is the sound of Mommy being wrong.

According to the friends with whom she stayed for five days, Rufus had a grand time. She liked the safe freedom she enjoyed around a more conventional house, not one perched on the edge of the woods like ours, where creatures great and small are likely to jump out of the bushes and grab you. She liked having the tiny dog to boss around; she liked having a large yard to de-insect all by herself. She even liked looking for a new place to lay her eggs, apparently her biggest concern.

Returning to the chicken yard she ignored the other chickens, including Agnes of God, and went straight to her nest, which it seemed she had been looking for the whole five days.

Agnes of God, for her part, far from running up to Rufus with sobs of relief and tales of the horrid behavior of the other girls, stayed on her nest, and merely looked over at Rufus as if to say "Oh, you're back."

So maybe she wasn't grieving. Maybe she was brooding. Broody. Sitting on her eggs and hoping they would hatch; they won't of course because there are no roosters around to fertilize them. Maybe when Rufus went away for a few days she saw her chance for a bit of tranquility.

As for Gertrude Stein, she seemed unintimidated by the bully's return. Mommy noticed as well that tiny pinfeathers at the back of her neck had started to grow.

Mommy had a good laugh at herself. Fiction Writers, and Poets, you know.

It reminded her of the epiphany she felt the first time she saw all of you eating a cracked egg and then playing with its shell. The one who had the piece of shell was chased down and tackled by all the others. And, while she held it in her beak, there was a lot of jumping up and down around her. This, Mommy thought, had to be how human ball games—football, baseball, soccer, basketball, etc.—began, since humans have learned so much of what we know from other animals. But maybe not.

Maybe earlier humans (Native Americans and Aboriginals excepted) didn't pay enough attention to animals to mimic their behavior, though Mommy, witnessing the ruin of the planet caused by human behavior, certainly wished they had.

Well, Mommies can be mistaken. Mommies, especially human Mommies, can be wrong. And there's a very good reason for this.

It is because human Mommies, like all Mommies on the planet, whether of fish or fowl, insect or reptile, are only surrogates. In fact, all creatures on the planet have the same parent.

You demonstrate this to Mommy every day. Because no matter how much you depend on the mash and grain Mommy provides, no matter how much you enjoy sitting and napping with her, the real excitement comes for you when she opens your gate and you are free to rush into your real mother's bounty. The bugs, the grasses, the seeds, the worms, the fallen apples and plums. It is She that you truly depend on, She whom you innately trust. Your love of Her is so hardwired in you, you probably don't even notice Her.

It is exactly the same with Mommy, who realizes that she is, like you, only small.

A tiny being hanging (though seeming to walk or even fly in planes) off the side of her Mother. For Mommy is not the same as Mother, and certainly not the same as The Mother. The one whose lap is too big to fall out of, whose head is too extraordinary to be fouled by chicken poop, whose mind is too flexible to worry about who gets eaten up and by what.

This Mother, unlike Mommy, never worries; time is her toy. Being is her thought.